D0591946

FACTS, MYTHS & MAYBES

Everything You Think You
Know About Catholicism,
But Perhaps Don't

FACTS, MYTHS & MAYBES

Everything You Think
You Know About Catholicism,
But Perhaps Don't

John Deedy

Thomas More
A Division of Tabor Publishing
Allen, Texas

Copyright © 1993 by John Deedy

All rights reserved. No part of this book shall be reproduced or transmitted in any form or by any means, electronic or mechanical, including photocopying, recording, or by any information or retrieval system, without written permission from the Publisher, Thomas More, a division of Tabor Publishing.

Send all inquiries to:
Tabor Publishing
200 East Bethany Drive
Allen, Texas 75002-3804

Printed in the United States of America

ISBN 0-88347-272-4

  2 3 4 5 6   98 97 96 95 94

For

    Kristine

    Tara

    Matthew

    Jon

    Garrett

    Paul

    John

the new generation

ABOUT THE AUTHOR

JOHN DEEDY is a veteran Catholic journalist and the author of a number of highly regarded books, including such Thomas More Press books as *The Catholic Fact Book, Retrospect: The Origins of Catholic Beliefs and Practices,* and *Matrix: Exploring the Challenges of Contemporary Life.* Among other publications, his work has appeared in the *New York Times,* the *Nation,* the *New Republic, The Critic* and *U.S. Catholic.*

CONTENTS

III

Religious Freedom, ''Deicide,'' Social Doctrine, Just-
War Theory, Annulments, Abortion, Birth Control,
Homosexuality, Suicide, Biotechnology, Euthanasia,
Living Wills, Cremation.

IV

Fast and Abstinence, Ember Days, Rogation Days,
Lent, Index of Forbidden Books, *Nihil Obstat/Imprima-
tur*, Miracles, Liberation Theology, Latin and the
Church, Cardinals/Monsignori, Stigmata, Dark Ages,
The Inquisition, Crusades, Medicine/Surgery (as prac-
ticed by priests and religious), Shroud of Turin, Santa
Claus, Christmas, Easter, Halloween, ''Boy-Bishop-
ing,'' Gregorian Calendar, Bells, Anti-Intellectualism,
Flat-Earth Theory, Evolution, Ecology, Masonry,
Rotary International, Knights of Columbus, Adam and
Eve and Navels, Patent Leather Shoes.

ACKNOWLEDGMENTS

Few researchers can get along without public libraries. I am grateful therefore for the assistance of the friendly folks at Sawyer Free Library in Gloucester and the Carnegie Library of Rockport, both in Massachusetts. As always, Cornelius M. Buckley and Father Paul F. Bailey were of help, both with ideas and information, and as sounding boards. So was Owen J. Murphy Jr. Father Lawrence McGrath of St. John's Seminary Library in Brighton, Massachusetts, helped clarify some points of Canon Law. Juli Peters DeLong of Catholic News Service's information department likewise was of assistance. My perspectives on Protestant theology were filtered through my Rockport friends, Ernest and Sharon Chace. Ernie was ordained a minister in the United Church of Christ; Sharon, a writer, artist and homemaker, attends theological seminary.

As with other books of mine of religious orientation, biblical quotes are in the main from the King James Version. In a few instances I have used quotes familiar to my childhood; these come from memory rather than any particular biblical translation. The King James Version is favored both for its beauty and, as we Catholics now acknowledge, its tradition.

FOREWORD

The Catholic Church is "semper eadem," always the same, never changing.

MYTH/FACT . . . It is impossible for anyone who remembers fish on Fridays, fasts before major feast days, fasting from midnight (even from water) on the day one went to communion, Latin Masses and the backs of priests saying Masses as if they were private devotions, to say the church doesn't change. The church does change. It is not *semper eadem*, always the same.

But, you counter, the cited changes are accidentals, matters of discipline not doctrine. Which seems true enough. Does it therefore follow that on matters of official teaching the church does not change? Well, let's take a look at that supposition.

There was the teaching that traveled under the phrase *extra ecclesiam nulla salus*—"outside the church, no salvation." From the third-century theology of Saint Cyprian; through *Unam sanctam*, the 1302 bull on papal supremacy by Pope Boniface VIII (1294-1303); through the profession of faith sworn by the Fathers of Vatican Council I (1869-1870): "This true Catholic Church, outside of which no one can be saved . . .''; through the 1930s and into the 1940s, when Boston Jesuit Father Leonard Feeney moved beyond ecumenics and invoked the phrase in condemnation of the white Anglo-Saxon Protestant community at Harvard, the Jewish community at Brandeis and sundry folks in between, *extra ecclesiam nulla salus* was official teaching. It was doctrine. The Catholic Church was the necessary means of salvation, and to gain heaven one had to be connected with it in some way. . . . But then along came Vatican Council II (1962-1965) and the Dogmatic Constitution on the Church, *Lumen gentium,* and suddenly the divine "plan of salvation" included others than just Catholics—in fact, the unbaptized as well as the baptized. Mighty change that.

There was also the ancient proscription against charging interest on loans of money. The twelfth canon of the first Council of Carthage (345) and the thirty-sixth canon of the Council of Aix (789) declared it reprehensible for laity to make money by lending at interest. Pope Benedict XIV (1740-1758) reaffirmed that position in the encyclical *Vix pervenit* of 1745, declaring that interest on loans was money unjustly claimed. Today there woudn't be a Vatican bank, a Catholic credit union or a diocesan lending office for its parishes, if the church had not changed.

Popes such as Gregory XVI (1831-1846) and Pius IX (1846-1878) held freedom of conscience to be beyond

Facts, Myths and Maybes

the pale of ecclesial acceptance; indeed, Gregory in 1834 even used the world *deliramentum,* delirium or insanity, in dismissing the notion of religious freedom. Yet *Dignitatis humanae,* Vatican II's Declaration on Religious Liberty, decreed: "It is one of the major tenets of Catholic doctrine that man's response to God in faith must be free . . . The church therefore is being faithful to the truth of the Gospel, and is following the way of Christ and the Apostles when she recognizes, and gives support to, the principle of religious freedom as befitting the dignity of man and as being in accord with divine revelation" (10-12).

One could go on, citing such details as slavery (the church long lived at spiritual and political peace with that dreadful institution), and the use of torture in pursuit of truth, and the banishment of "heathens" (ah, the burning of heretics, the Inquisition, the Crusades, the expulsion of the Moors from Spain). More currently there was the issue of the nature of the modern state. It was not until Jesuit Father John Courtney Murray was given a hearing that the church came to accept that not only could church and state be separate, but in that separateness resided potentially greater freedom and fuller theological health for the church itself.

So the church does change, perhaps slowly, perhaps imperceptibly, but change it does—and as Redemptorist Father Francis X. Murphy, *The New Yorker's*

John Deedy

Xavier Rynne of Vatican II, would add, in its "doctrinal, moral, disciplinary, and structural aspects." In other words, the whole ball of wax.

Or is "change" too blunt, too unnuanced a word?

Jesuit Father Avery Dulles uses the word *reconceptualization*. But maybe the first word, and the last, belongs better to John Henry Cardinal Newman. The word is *development*, and it's straight from the title of the work he wrote during the two years (1843-1845) before leaving Anglicanism for Roman Catholicism: "Essay on the Development of Doctrine." Applying the principle of life as the test of truth in religion, Newman argued that as in the body there are changes which are anything but corruptions, so in the church there are changes in which old principles reappear under new forms. The church "changes with them in order to remain the same." In a higher world, it might be otherwise, Newman conceded, "but here below to live is to change and to be perfect is to have changed often."

In other words, as English Jesuit George Hayward Joyce said early in the century, Newman showed how a true and fertile idea is endowed with a vital and assimilative energy of its own, "in virtue of which, without undergoing the least substantive change, it attains an ever completer expression, as the course of time brings it in contact with new aspects of truth or forces it into collision with new errors." The life of an idea, then, is analogous to an organic development. As an organ develops, so does the church, "enlarging the range and refining the sense of her teaching."

That last quote is Newman's, and special note is called to it, for it sets the tone for much of this book.

This book is not formal history, nor is it apologia, nor is it an attempt at systematic and exhaustive presentation of the dogma, teaching and tradition of the universal Catholic Church, although there are elements of all in the book. The book is divided into four sections representing four currents of faith—doctrine, morals and ethics, worship, culture and tradition—and purports to be no more than its title, a collection of facts, myths and maybes about the Catholic Church— "maybes," because there are items of belief for which the church does not have solid, unequivocal explanations; e.g., Limbo.

My editorial tack is to take the more common tenets, thoughts, feelings, suppositions and opinions of and about the church, set them forth in the form of statement (per this foreward), then examine them—you guessed it—as fact, myth or maybe . . . or combination thereof.

If at times the book seems irreverent, skeptical, credulous, tentative or a host things more, it is because like Newman, I regard the church as something of a organism, (micro or macro, as the case may be) in a vital, but also developing process, one in which the character of the whole and of its innumerable parts is in constant shaping and reshaping.

Which translates quite simply: the church changes even as we read these pages. Hence, here there are no concluding chapters.

John Deedy
Rockport, Massachusetts
Spring, 1992

P.S.—As this book was being completed, the International Commision on English in the Liturgy (ICEL) was circulating to the U.S. and other English-speaking bishops' conferences a proposed new English translation of the mass, involving changes in the Nicene Creed and the Our Father, among other prayers. Most of the changes relate to gender-inclusive language. Because the revised texts were not expected to be approved and sent out by the ICEL to English-speaking bishops' conferences before June 1994, it was not possible to include them in the relevant sections of this book. The U.S. bishops could not discuss the new texts and vote on them before November 1994, at the earliest.

I

Doctrine

Doctrine equates to the embodiment or substance of faith. It is the sum of what the church teaches and must be believed on divine authority. Doctrine begins with belief in one God, who is pure spirit, transcendent and supreme; who is the creator of Heaven and earth, and possessor of the highest attributes. This God is all holy, all wise, all loving, all knowing, all just, all merciful, all powerful. Through Jesus Christ, God incarnate, God ordained a faith and a church based on revealed truths —that is, truths contained in Scripture or in Tradition, or both, and which would be preserved over time in that church's ordinary teaching and definitions. Doctrine, then, proceeds from belief in God to belief in particulars.

17

John Deedy

The basic code summing up the fundamental obligations of religion and morality, including that of the Catholic Church and of Catholics themselves, is an inheritance from the Old Testament in the form of the Ten Commandments.

FACT . . . The Ten Commandments, or Decalogue, do indeed comprise the church's basic moral code, and Christian belief is that the Commandments come from God, although not through Jesus Christ, but rather Moses. The Commandments were written, the Scriptures relate, by the finger of God on two tablets of stone, then received by Moses on Mount Sinai. Moses made them the basis of Mosaic Law, and Christ in turn embraced them completely: "If you will enter into life, keep the Commandments" (Matthew 19:17).

The Commandments are twice recorded in the Pentateuch (the first five books of the Old Testament): in Exodus and in Deuteronomy. Christ alluded to them frequently in the New Testament, and summarized them in the double precept of charity: love of God and love of neighbor. Christianity adopted the Ten Commandments with only one notable variation—the day of the week to be kept holy, according to the Third Commandment. Christianity changed it from the last day of the week (Saturday), to the first (Sunday).

The first three Commandments concern the individual's relationship to God; the other seven, the individual's relationship with neighbor. All Ten Commandments are conditioned by love—the first three love of God directly; the others, the love which in the ideal order should flow to family and neighbor through love of God, thereby becoming the basis for justice among peoples.

The Ten Commandments are as follows:
1. I am the Lord, your God, you shall not have other gods before you (Exodus 20:2-3);
2. You shall not take the name of the Lord, your God, in vain (Exodus 20:7);
3. Remember to keep holy the Sabbath Day (Exodus 20:12);
4. Honor your father and your mother (Exodus 20:12);
5. You shall not kill (Exodus 20:13);
6. You shall not commit adultery (Exodus 20:14);
7. You shall not steal (Exodus 20:15);
8. You shall not bear false witness against your neighbor (Exodus 20:16);
9. You shall not covet your neighbor's wife (Exodus 20:17);
10. You shall not covet your neighbor's house (Exodus 20:17).

The Beatitudes expostulated by Christ in the Sermon on the Mount are sometimes described as the positive application of the Commandments. In contrast to the Commandments, which are essentially admonishing,

John Deedy

the Beatitudes are hortatory. Also, whereas the Commandments address what is necessary to live according to the law of God, the Beatitudes speak of the happiness that is possible on earth as well as in Heaven for those who live by their precepts of love and charity.

* * *

The Beatitudes come in variant versions.

FACT . . . There are two versions of that portion of Christ's Sermon on the Mount, known as the Beatitudes: The Beatitudes according to Matthew (5:3-10) and those according to Luke (6:20-23). Matthew's is the more popular and the longer version, containing eight declarations of blessedness to Luke's four. In the older and more familiar translations, the two versions follow.

Matthew's:

—Blessed are the poor in spirit: for theirs is the Kingdom of Heaven;
—Blessed are they that mourn: for they shall be comforted;
—Blessed are the meek: for they shall inherit the earth;
—Blessed are they who hunger and thirst after justice: for they shall be filled;

20

—Blessed are the merciful: for they shall obtain mercy;

—Blessed are the pure in heart: for they shall see God;

—Blessed are the peacemakers: for they shall be called the children of God;

—Blessed are they who suffer persecution for justice's sake: for theirs is the Kingdom of Heaven.

Luke's:

—Blessed are the poor: for yours is the Kingdom of Heaven;

—Blessed are you who hunger now: for you shall be satisfied;

—Blessed are you who weep now: for you shall laugh;

—Blessed are you when men shall hate you, and when they shut you out, and reproach you, and reject your name as evil, because of the Son of Man. Rejoice on that day and exult, for behold your reward is great in Heaven.

*   *   *

The Trinity is the cornerstone of Catholic faith.

TRUE . . . The Trinity is indeed the cornerstone of faith, in the sense that it is the dogma upon which the whole of Catholic Christian belief is constructed. It is the central dogma of the Catholic religion.

In sum, the Trinity is the dogma that in the unity of the Godhead there are three persons, the Father, Son and Holy Spirit; that these three persons are truly distinct from one another, yet at the same time one in the same divine essence. In this Trinity of persons, the Father is unbegotten, the Son is begotten by an eternal generation, and the Holy Spirit proceeds from the Father and the Son by an eternal procession. Each person of the Trinity is separate from the other, yet once again, Father, Son and Holy Spirit together comprise only one God. The three persons are co-eternal and co-equal. Each is uncreated; each is omnipotent.

The Trinity is a mystery of faith. Its understanding eludes created intelligence.

* * *

The Trinity is an evolved doctrine of Christianity.

FALSE . . . It is true that the Trinity has been challenged as a second-century formulation which did not receive final approbation until the fourth century. It is true, too, that some sought to account for the Trinity as a Christian reflex of an imaginary law of nature inducing peoples to group their objects of worship into sets of three.

Catholic theology counters that the Trinity was

clearly foreshadowed in the Old Testament (Gen. 1:16; 3:22; 11:7; Num. 6:23-26; Is. 6:1-9, etc.), and explicitly proclaimed in the New Testament, as when Christ bade the Apostles to teach all nations, ''baptizing them in the name of the Father, and of the Son, and of the Holy Ghost'' (Matt. 28:19), and when he taught that ''when the Comforter is come, whom I shall send unto you from the Father, even the Spirit of Truth, which pro- ceedeth from the Father, he shall testify of me'' (John 15:26). Also cited are Matt. 3:16; 10:21; 17:5; Luke 4:18; John 3:35; 2 Cor. 13:13; 1 John 5:17, etc.

The Trinity in its understanding of a Godhead of three persons in one is an essential of Catholic Chris- tianity, but the principle is hardly a universal one. Monotheism is an antecedent to belief in the Trinity, but Judaism of course does not accept the Trinity, and neither does Islam. Unitarians reject the Trinity by the mere fact of not accepting the divinity of Christ, and Swedenborgians interpret the Trinity not as three distinct divine persons, but as a grouping in which divinity centers in the Incarnate Christ.

The Catholic Church honors the Trinity throughout the year, but especially on Trinity Sunday (the first Sunday after Pentecost), a feast originating in the four- teenth century, and in its everyday prayer life with the doxology (prayer of praise), ''Glory be to the Father, and to the Son, and to the Holy Spirit, as it was in the beginning, is now, and ever shall be, world without end." That doxology was common among Christians as early as the fourth century.

*   *   *

The clearest statement of the Trinity is continued in the Nicene Creed recited at every Mass everywhere in the world.

FACT . . . More than that, the Nicene Creed is the embodiment of the Catholic Christian belief itself. If anyone asks a Catholic what he or she believes, the essentials are all there in the Creed, recited as the profession of faith immediately after the homily, as follows:

We believe in one God, the Father, the Almighty, maker of heaven and earth, of all that is seen and unseen.

We believe in one Lord, Jesus Christ, the only Son of God, eternally begotten of the Father, God from God, Light from Light, true God from true God, begotten, not made, one in being with the Father. Through him all things were made.

For us men and for our salvation he came down from heaven: by the power of the Holy Spirit he was born of the Virgin Mary, and became man.

For our sake he was crucified under Pontius Pilate; he suffered, died, and was buried. On the third day he rose again in fulfillment of the Scriptures; he ascended into heaven and is seated at the right hand of the Father. He will come again in glory to judge the living and the dead, and his kingdom will have no end.

We believe in the Holy Spirit, the Lord, the giver of life, who proceeds from the Father and the Son. With the Father and the Son he is worshipped and glorified. He has spoken through the prophets.

We believe in one holy catholic and apostolic church. We acknowledge one baptism for the forgiveness of sins. We look for the resurrection of the dead, and the life of the world to come. Amen.

* * *

The schism between East and West resulted from the Nicene Creed's "filioque" clause.

TRUE . . . although other issues certainly aggravated the situation, such as geography (Who had claim as the true depository of Graeco-Roman civilization, the East or West?) and the precedence of the patriarchs of the major centers of civilization: Rome, Constantinople, Alexandria, Antioch, Jerusalem (Were the patriarchs equal in rank? Was one first among equals? Did one enjoy primacy over the others?).

But the critical issues most definitely were theological—that of Purgatory, for one, but more specifically that of *filioque*, the "and the Son" clause which Rome inserted into the Nicene Creed, thus giving doctrinal expression to belief in the double procession of the Holy Spirit from the Father as well as the Son. The East regarded the insertion as a tampering with orthodox faith, and responded at the synod of Constantinople presided over by the Patriarch Photius in 867 by excommunicating the pope, Nicholas I. Photius was deposed, then rehabilitated, but the stage was set for a full-blown schism and complete separation.

The *filioque* matter was no new issue in 867. It had been festering since the reign of Leo III (795-816), with Spanish and Frankish theologians the strong proponents of the *filioque* idea. Though Leo agreed with the theology, he questioned the propriety of the addition of *filioque* to the Creed. Several succeeding popes felt likewise, but not Sergius IV (1009-1012). On his election, he took the decisive step. He included a copy of the Nicene Creed incorporating the *filioque* clause with the customary announcement containing a new pope's profession of faith which was to be sent the Patriarch of Constantinople. The patriarch refused thereupon to recognize Sergius' election and he excommunicated him. It was the true beginning of the East-West schism, although the breach would not become final until some years later.

The climatic incident was fomented by a delegation

sent to Constantinople by Leo IX (1049-1054), ostensibly in conjunction with initiatives of the Emperor to settle the controversy and bring about a reconciliation. The Roman delegation was headed by Cardinal Humbert of Silva Candida, who, it is recorded, conducted himself with "tactless arrogance." The Patriarch of Constantinople was now Michael Cerularius. Cerularius refused to accept Humbert's letter of presentation, or bull, among other reasons because it expressed doubt about the legitimacy of his elevation. Stung by the refusal, Humbert lashed out, offending Eastern sensibilities with a series of insulting actions, including an attack on Greek Christians for rejecting *filioque* theology. In a culminating gesture, Humbert deposited on the high altar of the Hagia Sophia, the famed church, now a mosque, built by Justinian, a bull of excommunication beginning: "Let God witness and judge. . . ." The date was July 16, 1054.

Michael Cerularius countered by convoking a synod, which condemned Humbert and his bull, and excommunicated him and his party.

For Rome the schism was now fact. In the East, however, division was not accepted as final until the diverting of the Fourth Crusade, the cruel sacking of Constantinople, and Innocent III's establishment in 1204 of a Latin Empire of Constantinople, complete with Latin-rite patriarch. Innocent (1198-1216) thought the Latin patriarchate would help in the reunion of the churches of East and West. To the East it was the last straw.

* * *

For Catholics, as for all people, the primary guiding norm in matters of right and wrong is the conscience of the individual.

FACT . . . Although the point is considerably obfuscated by Catholic emphases on authority and claims of precedence favoring the magisterium.

Conscience, by way of definition, is the intrinsic faculty by which an individual arrives at a judgment concerning the rightness or wrongness of a particular act. Historically the church had honored the primacy of conscience, while at the same time holding that the best-formed conscience was one aided by good will, right use of the emotions, experience of living, and certain other external helps. Chief among the latter was, of course, the authoritative teaching office of the church —the magisterium or teaching authority.

Fine, except there's an obvious dichotomy.

Conscience is the "voice of reason" or "voice of God," and in Catholic understanding a person who follows/obeys the dictates of conscience does not offend God. On the other hand, Catholic understanding ties conscience to obedience, and indeed exalts obedience to a virtue when the individual subjects his/her will to that of another for God's sake. In other words, conscience is absolute, but conscience is also subject to obedience.

The dichotomy does not end there.

The church so respects conscience that it holds free from guilt a wrongful act arising from a certain but erroneous conscience. This is not to say that the wrongful act is itself made good by the erroneous conscience, but rather that the individual is not held responsible for the wrongful act because the conscience knows no better. That point is underscored by Vatican II's Pastoral Constitution on the Church in the Modern World, *Gaudium et spes:* "Conscience frequently errs from invincible ignorance without losing its dignity" (16.)

The other side of the coin is that because conscience by itself can err, the church insists that consciences be properly formed. What one is talking about then is a "correct conscience"—that is, one which is in harmony with church teaching. The position of the leadership is that the individual Catholic is responsible for knowing the position of the church, and conforming her/his conscience to that position.

The obvious difficulty is, what happens if on "knowing" the position of the church and thoughtfully weighing its reasoning, one's conscience rejects that position? Does the authority of the magisterium then take precedence over the demands of conscience? Despite all the pronouncements that a "good Catholic" does not dissent from the magisterium, the answer is no. Conscience has the claim of ascendancy.

* * *

A doubtful conscience can render a Catholic morally indecisive, and unable to act one way or another.

MYTH . . . If, after attempts to resolve a doubtful conscience, the conscience remains doubtful regarding the morality of a particular action, the doubt may be settled by the invocation of probabilism. Probabilism is a system of moral and pastoral theology which holds that, where there is a question of an act's lawfulness or unlawfulness, licitness or illicitness, it is permissible to follow a geniunely probable opinion in favor of liberty, providing of course the position is truly and solidly probable, even though the opposing position may be more probable.

* * *

Catholic understanding of conscience, then, is a variable.

WRONG . . . It sometimes might seem so, given debates of recent years over moral issues and the claims and counterclaims, abuses and assertions, of peoples within the church. Nonetheless, the official position of the church with regard to conscience remains constant.

Facts, Myths and Maybes

To sum up, individuals are obliged (1) to obey a certain and correct conscience; (2) to obey a certain conscience even when it is erroneous out of ignorance; (3) to disregard and correct a conscience known to be erroneous or derelict; (4) to rectify a scrupulous conscience, which sees error where there is none; (5) to resolve a doubtful conscience, if possible, before acting.

These conditions apply in all matters of law, evolved and natural.

*   *   *

The Natural Law is a concept unique to Catholicism.

MYTH . . . Although one could easily have thought so at the time of U.S. Senate confirmation hearings on Clarence Thomas and reaction to the future Supreme Court justice's expressions of esteem for Natural Law. It was, said the *New York Times,* almost as if "the man had let slip a reference to torture by thumbscrews" or "had disclosed an obscure and probably sinister belief in alchemy."

The fact is that Natural Law as philosophical and theological theory existed before Christianity itself. Socrates, Plato and Aristotle propounded concepts of Natural Law, while Roman Law recognized Natural Law as the ultimate test of the reasonableness of positive law. To be sure, Saint Paul wrote in Romans 2:14 that the Natural Law is written in the human heart

31

John Deedy

("For when Gentiles, which have not the law, do by nature the things contained in the law, these, having not the law, are a law unto themselves.") But then too Locke, Montesquieu, Jefferson, Adams, Lincoln and more recently Martin Luther King Jr. all invoked Natural Law in the interests of human rights issues and racial equality. Natural Law, in sum, has been around as long as reason.

Believers in a force beyond self and nature define Natural Law as the law which is imprinted in the hearts and minds of people. As such Natural Law is both participation and reflection in the rational individual of the law of God. By extension Natural Law becomes an expression in rational beings of the very essence of God. This law is called natural because it can be perceived by reason alone; in other words, its precepts can be deduced by objective right reasoning totally on the basis of data derived of human nature. Natural Law, in other words, is not a product of social agreement, convention or legislative process. Accordingly, Natural Law is antecedent to positive law, human and divine, and is the law to which other precepts spelling out obligations and responsibilities are attached. The Ten Commandments then are written expressions of Natural Law, with the exception of the Third. The precepts of charity—love of God and love of neighbor—also belong to Natural Law.

Natural Law, finally, is universal and immutable. By

way of example, murder is always and everywhere inherently wrong because it is a violation of Natural Law; so is polyandry; so is slavery. By contrast, driving the wrong way on a one-way street is wrong, but it is a civil wrong, a violation of human or conventional law, not of Natural Law; a Catholic's neglecting to receive the Eucharist during Eastertime is a wrong, but it is an ecclesial wrong, a violation of church precept, not of Natural Law.

The problem with Natural Law is that it is not always obvious, with the result that much that is debatable is often claimed in its name. In Catholicism, for instance, official teaching holds artificial birth control to be a violation of Natural Law since the natural functions of the reproductive organs are frustrated or perverted by sexual vice; this is a view widely contested by theological and scientific opinion, much of it Catholic.

There's the additional problem that Natural Law seems to speak to some people differently than others. For instance, Catholic theology holds abortion to be in contravention to Natural Law, but not all Jewish and Protestant theological thought would be in agreement.

For some this dichotomy brings into question the premise of an order governing the material universe infused with a law which can be ascertained and agreed upon by all. Apparently it can't. But does this mean that Natural Law is reeling or dead? Not at all. As the

John Deedy

New York Times recently quoted Princeton University professor Robert P. George, "natural law theory is very much alive and well." We live by it.

* * *

As the fundamental source of doctrine for Roman Catholicism—as well as, of course, for Protestantism, Anglican Christianity, Eastern Orthodoxy and Judaism—the Bible has always enjoyed a special place in the hearths and hearts of Catholics, from pope to peasant.

MYTH . . . The Bible is indeed the Catholic Church's fundamental source of doctrine. Its two Testaments of seventy-three books, forty-six in the Old and twenty-seven in the New, are regarded as the inspired Word of God, though the whole did not arrive among believers full-blown and air-tight, written by the finger of God and carved in stone like the Ten Commandments that Moses received on Mount Sinai. The Bible was written in separate fragments and over several centuries' time before being drawn together into a single book. Nonetheless, the Bible is the key to everything that Catholicism is about, its word(s) so sacred that everyone who proclaimed them was admonished to utter first a prayer of worthiness—a ritual that endures to this day in the prayer the celebrant of Mass speaks silently immediately before the Gospel: "Cleanse my heart and my lips, Almighty God, that I may worthily

34

and becomingly announce thy holy Gospel." (Some priests speak the prayer aloud, as if to join the congregation in the petition, but theirs is a liturgical liberty.)

The Bible being so holy a book, one would expect the Catholic Church to have been forever championing its place on every Catholic reading list. It does now, but that's a change. For several centuries the Bible was both bane and blessing for the Catholic Church. It was on no Catholic's reading table—or relatively few, at least. The Bible might have been in the home, but it collected dust. It had come to be regarded as something of a dangerous instrument. Rome was perfectly satisfied that it be unread. There would be no vacuum. Rome would pass on its interpretation of its contents, and the faithful would be guided accordingly.

This situation grew out of the extraordinary interest in the Bible enkindled by the Reformation and the Reformation's favoring of private interpretation of the contents of the Bible. In Rome this notion was anathema, and ultimately the church was put at odds with itself. What developed was that at the same time the church was encouraging Catholics to read the Bible, it was warning against reading it, lest the faithful depart from Rome's official interpretation of chapter and verse.

In Protestantism, in the meanwhile, the Bible had become not only an indispensable tool of personal salvation, but also an instrument of proselytism. Bible societies mushroomed, and assiduous missionaries fanned out distributing Bibles by the hundreds of thousands in country after country. Rome's upset was palpable. Denominational lines were being crossed, and by people who were circulating Bibles that (1) were without note or comment, or (2) with notes and commentary neither cleared nor approved by Rome as self-proclaimed "divinely appointed custodian and interpreter of Holy Writ."

Predictably there were warnings and condemnations.

In 1824 Pope Leo XII (1823-1829) wrote the bishops of the world in the encyclical *Ubi primum:* "You are aware, venerable brothers, that a certain bible society is imprudently spreading throughout the world, which, despising the tradition of the holy Fathers and the decree of the Council of Trent, is endeavoring to translate, or rather to pervert the Scriptures into the vernacular of all nations. . . . It is to be feared that by false interpretation, the Gospel of Christ will become the gospel of men, or still worse, the gospel of evil."

Pius IX (1846-1878) echoed the admonition in the encyclical *Qui pluribus,* to wit: "These crafty bible societies, which renew the ancient guile of heretics, cease not to thrust their bibles upon all men, even the unlearned—their bibles, which have been translated against the laws of the church, and often contain false explanations of the text. Thus the divine traditions, the

Facts, Myths and Maybes

teaching of the fathers, and the authority of the Catholic Church are rejected, and everyone in his own way interprets the words of the Lord, and distorts their meaning, thereby falling into miserable error.''

The din was insistent. Pius VIII (1829-1830) and Gregory XVI (1831-1846) sounded warnings, and in 1897 the Holy Congregation of the Index forbade further research into the origin of biblical texts.

The cumulative result was inculcation of the idea among Catholics that Bible reading was not a fully approved practice. Hence the phenomenon of the Bible becoming the great unread book in Roman Catholicism, including the Catholic homes having a so-called approved version.

The mood began to change during the reign of Leo XIII (1878-1903). In 1893 Leo issued the encyclical *Providentissimus Deus* encouraging the practice of reading and pious reflection on the Bible, and in 1898 he granted an indulgence of three hundred days to those who read the Gospels for at least fifteen minutes. The road was marked. In 1909, Pius X established the Pontifical Biblical Institute, and his successors, Benedict XV (1914-1922), Pius XI (1922-1939) and Pius XII (1939-1958), virtually vied with one another in heralding the Bible. In fact, Pius XII's 1943 encyclical *Divino afflante Spiritu* became seminal in the promotion of biblical studies.

Actions and documents such as these so changed

moods that today we have interconfessional Bibles and no more hang-ups over niceties of ecclesiastical protocol. For most, the Bible is the Bible.

In the process, the Bible has been rehabilitated among the Catholic rank-and-file. A 1987 survey showed that the number of Catholics who said they had read the Bible within the last thirty days had risen from 23 percent in 1977 to 32 percent in 1986. At the same time, however, only 21 percent of Catholics said that reading or studying the Bible was "very important" to them, in contrast to 52 percent of Protestants and 85 percent of those who described themselves as Evangelicals.

The Bible, then, is achieving a place of honor among Catholics. But obviously there's a distance to go before for Catholics in the pew, the Bible is the "catholic" book it was up to the Reformation, before it was "coopted" by the reformers and defaulted on by Rome.

* * *

Catholic detachment from the Bible can be explained in context of the book's ineffable mysteries.

MYTH . . . It is fiction that there was or is something ineffable about the Bible for Catholics—in other words, that it is almost too holy to read. Yet that case was made by apologists right up to Vatican Council II (1962-1965). For instance, as a young bishop, the future Cardinal

Facts, Myths and Maybes

John Wright contended Catholics were not well-versed in the Scripture because they viewed the Bible less as a book to be read familiarly and often, than as a compendium of sacred mysteries to be regarded with distance, reverence and holy awe. Thus, as with Jews, certain words were ineffable and therefore too sacred to speak (hence Adonai for Yahweh or Jehovah), so presumably with Catholics was the Bible too sacred to be picked up and indulged in (hence, among other things, the popularity of books of meditation like Thomas a Kempis' *The Imitation of Christ*).

Perhaps the best answer to the apologists was provided by Flannery O'Connor, the Southern Catholic writer. "Catholics who are not articulate about their love of the Bible," O'Connor wrote in answer to Wright, "are generally those who do not love it since they read it as seldom as possible, and those who do not read the Bible do not because of laziness or indifference or the fear that reading it will endanger their faith, not the Catholic faith but faith itself."

The rejoinder is quoted by Professor Ralph C. Wood in *The Flannery O'Connor Bulletin* for 1976, an annual published by Georgia College in Milledgeville. In fact, said Wood, for Flannery O'Connor, "The empty faith of liberalism and the candied piety of conservatism both have their origin . . . in the church's massive ignorance of the Bible."

* * *

39

John Deedy

Parts of the Bible are hard to take seriously, as for instance Methuselah's living 969 years (Genesis 5:27) and the Red Sea's parting for Moses and the Israelites (Exodus 14:15-30).

TRUE . . . except it is now almost everywhere conceded that the Bible makes use of myths, legends and symbols—storytelling, if you will—and is not to be taken literally in its every word and phrase. This is especially true of the Old Testament and certain events related there, including the two of the statement, although exegetes are able to find explanations for each of the above.

Methuselah's age might have been calculated by a system different from our own—common enough once upon a time. If, for instance, the calculation was by full moons rather than years, Methuselah would have lived to be eighty years, seven months—ripe old age, but possible then as now, and a sufficiently long time to dramatize Genesis' point with respect to longevity.

Similarly, concerning the parting of the Red Sea. Researchers have offered a number of explanations for this improbable event, among them that the flight from Pharoah's army was through the marshy Sea of Reeds rather than the present-day Red Sea. A more novel theory was offered in 1992 by two prominent ocean-ographers writing in the *Bulletin of the American Meteorological Society.* They argued that because of the peculiar topography of the Gulf of Suez, a northwest

Facts, Myths and Maybes

wind of 46-miles-per-hour blowing steadily for ten hours could cause a ten-foot drop in the sea level at the gulf's northern end, exposing the sea floor for passage on foot. At the same time, a sudden change in wind direction would allow the waters to rush back in an engulfing wave—as Exodus indeed says happened, drowning the Israelites' pursuers. (There's the problem that Exodus says the wind was from the East, but the oceanographers say that could have been a deceptive variant local wind created by nearby mountains. The dominant winds of the area are from the northwest.).

So no one knows for sure—but explanations do seem to be available for seemingly extravagant Biblical accounts.

As for the church, for centuries it accepted the Bible at its word, despite the attacks and mockeries of rationalists. Credulousness became impossible, however, with the scientific breakthroughs of the nineteenth century, as in the field of evolution. Religion had to concede that the Bible was not a literal account in toto of the events described therein. Pope Leo XIII (1878-1903) made the church's concession in the 1893 encyclical, *Providentissimus Deus.*

Leo offered a strong defense of the inerrancy of the Bible, but granted that "a certain religious obscurity" may surround certain passages of the Scriptures. Not to worry. "The sacred writers," he wrote, ". . . did

John Deedy

not seek to penetrate the secrets of nature, but rather described and dealt with things in more or less figurative language, or in terms which were commonly used at the time.''

Vatican Council II (1962-1965) echoed the point in *Dei verbum,* its Dogmatic Constitution on Revelation: ''The interpreter must investigate what meaning the sacred writer intended to express and actually expressed in particular circumstances as he used contemporary literary forms in accordance with the situation of his own time and culture. For the correct understanding of what the sacred author wanted to assert, due attention must be paid to the customary and characteristic styles of perceiving, speaking, and narrating which prevailed at the time of the sacred writer, and to the customs men normally followed at that period in their everyday dealings with one another.'' (12)

That's counsel for the professional exegete. As for the people in the pew, it's perhaps enough to be assured that the Bible remains the authentic record of God's revelation in history. The church is adamant about that.

* * *

The polytheistic religion of the Greeks and Romans included gods who were female as well as male, but the God of the monotheistic Christian faith is a male God only.

42

Facts, Myths and Maybes

MAYBE . . . To be sure, the Greeks and the Romans included females in their pantheons of gods. Hera was the Greeks' queen of heaven; her counterpart, Juno, was for Romans the principle of life. Minerva was the Roman goddess of the arts and sciences; Athena, the Greek goddess of wisdom and prudent warfare; Hestia and Vesta, the Greek and Roman goddesses, respectively, of the hearth. The list goes on. The argument is made that elimination of females from the ranks of the gods inexorably contributed to gender discrimination in religion and to the male chauvinism of monotheism, including Christianity. It is a seductive argument, except it is not at all certain that the lot of ancient Greek and Roman women was any better under their religious systems of polytheism than was to prove the case for women under a monotheistic male god.

As for the God of Christianity, it is true that maleness predominates. The second person of the Trinity, the incarnate God whom we know as Jesus Christ, was, of course, male, and the God whom he invoked in heaven was invariably a male God. Using the Aramaic form *abba*, Jesus spoke repeatedly of "my Father," not mother, and when he asked his followers to pray with confidence, that prayer began with the words, "Our Father, who art in heaven" (Matt. 6:9). There are any number of instances more of Jesus' male directiveness; for instance, the request of forgiveness directed from

43

the cross was "Father, forgive them, for they know not what they do" (Luke 23:34). There was no female in any of this, no mother, no she.

On the other hand, there is the third person of the Trinity, the God of the Holy Spirit, and in the Old Testament the Holy Spirit is often alluded to in the feminine gender—a detail which accounts for the Holy Spirit being at the heart of current developments in feminine spirituality. The feminine references to the Holy Spirit are most specific in the book of Wisdom, as when Solomon petitions God: "Send her forth from your holy heavens and from your glorious throne dispatch her that she may be with me and work with me, that I may know what is your pleasure. For she knows and understands all things, and will guide me discreetly in my affairs, and safeguard me by her glory" (Wis. 9:10-11).

Further, the Old Testament frequently portrays the Godhead in feminine gender, including as a mother in the book of Isaiah. There the Lord goes forth exclaiming, "Now will I cry like a travailing woman" (42:14), and later the Lord promises that "As one whom his mother comforteth, so will I comfort you" (66:13).

A lately acquired sensitivity to these and other feminine references in Scripture has prompted some theologians to break with old traditions and begin to speak of God as "she" as well as "he." They defend the usage on the additional grounds that it acknowledges

44

more fully the fullness of God as mirrored in creatures, male *and female,* created in the ''image of God.''

In their book *How to Save the Catholic Church* (Viking 1984), Andrew M. Greeley and Mary Greeley Durkin propose woman as an analog of God, contending that God cannot be comprehended adequately by a people who use only masculine imagery of God. They then confront the gender issue with a series of pointed questions and answers: ''Is God male or female? God combines the equal perfections of both. Does God love like a mother or like a father? God loves in ways that are reflected equally by the two packages of human loving. Can we call God She? Every bit as much as we can call her He . . . God is both a mother and a father.''

* * *

Catholicism doesn't need a feminine God, or even a feminine concept of God, because in Catholicism, Mary is a surrogate God.

FALSE . . . Indeed, Mary enjoys a unique place in Catholic Christianity, and devotion to her has been strong in Catholic Christianity since at least the second century. Over centuries she has occupied the thoughts of liturgists, captured the imaginations of mystics, poets, artists and explorers, and been an object of devotion of almost supernatural dimension among the Catholic faithful. But this is and always has been in

45

the role of Mother of God, not as a surrogate god, much less as a god in her own right.

Devotion to Mary seems to have been instinctive among early Christians. It was propelled through history, not by the wonders of miracles and apparitions, but by theological concepts of her as a counterpart to Eve, Mary's role in the Redemption remedying Eve's role in the Fall of humankind in the Garden of Eden. Like so much else in Marian theology, the contrast between Eve the temptress and Mary the instrument for Redemption is easily strained. Nonetheless, Mary figures in Catholicism as a kind of second Eve, the epitome of the new first mother; in sum, the perfect woman.

Mary was never worshipped as a god or goddess, however, and she isn't now. There have been frequent efforts to have Mary declared co-redeemer with Christ of humankind, but as much as she has always been revered in Catholic Christianity, the notion of placing her on the same exalted pedestal as her son has remained foreign to the church's instincts. It has been enough that she stand forth as model and exemplar of the totally virtuous woman.

In Catholic devotional understanding, adoration belongs to God alone. Mary, then, is venerated, as the angels and saints are also venerated. In the fine print of Catholic theology, veneration is known as *dulia*.

Facts, Myths and Maybes

Mary, however, is accorded *hyperdulia,* because she is above the angels and saints. But she is still not God.

* * *

Mary was born free of Original Sin.

TRUE . . . Mary was born free of Original Sin, and this is the event Catholics know as the Immaculate Conception.

There is confusion among Catholics about this doctrine, the common tendency being to mix it up with that of the Virgin Birth. The two are quite different concepts.

The process by which Jesus was born is known as the Virgin Birth. Which is to say, Jesus was born of Mary without Mary losing her virginity. Jesus, in a word, was conceived of the Holy Ghost, not of man— or more specifically, not of Mary's spouse Joseph. Conceiving miraculously, Mary remained a virgin in birth. This ancient teaching was restated by Pope John Paul II in the encyclical *Redemptoris Mater,* the pope's commenting that Mary "preserved her virginity intact." The comment is discreet, and consistent with traditional Catholic teaching that in giving birth to Jesus three phenomena occurred: Mary's hymen remained intact, the birth was painless, and there was no afterbirth *(sordes).* Tradition deriving from the teaching of

John Deedy

Saints Jerome, Augustine, Ambrose and John Chrysostom, among others, holds further that Mary remained a virgin throughout the rest of her life. That latter detail, important as it historically has been for certain Catholic sensibilities, is not crucial to the doctrine of the Virgin Birth.

By contrast, the doctrine of the Immaculate Conception relates to Mary's birth, not Jesus'.

Mary was conceived in normal copulative manner by her parents, Saints Anne and Joachim. However, as the one predestined to bear the savior into the world, Mary "in the first instant of her conception was, by a singular grace and privilege of Almighty God in view of the merits of Jesus Christ the Saviour of the human race, preserved exempt from all stain of original sin." As said, this exemption from Original Sin is the doctrine of the Immaculate Conception; the quote is from Pope Pius IX's bull of 1854, *Ineffabilis Deus,* declaring the doctrine a matter of faith and morals, its belief binding on all Catholics.

In pronouncing the doctrine, Pius IX held that, "It was altogether becoming that as the Only Begotten had a Father in Heaven whom the seraphim extol as thrice holy, so he should have a mother on earth who should never lack the splendor of holiness."

Original Sin—the sin of Adam and Eve for eating of the forbidden fruit, and passed on to all humans—is removed through baptism. Catholic teaching is that Mary is the only human ever exempted from that first, Original Sin.

*   *   *

As the successor of the apostle Peter, and the person in a direct link to Jesus Christ, the pope is the Vicar of Christ.

MAYBE . . . The pope has many titles, among them Bishop of Rome, Successor of Saint Peter, Prince of the Apostles, Supreme Pontiff of the Universal Church, Patriarch of the West, Primate of Italy, Archbishop and Metropolitan of the Roman Province, Sovereign of Vatican City, Servant of the Servants of God. But the most august title of all is that of Vicar of Christ. The problem is that the title is of Middle-Ages origin, and thus a belated claim. Some feel it may actually be a dangerous exaggeration of authority and persona.

In the early church, bishops commonly identified themselves as vicars of Christ, but the honorific was not assumed by popes as their special entitlement until the eighth century, when Vicar of Christ began to supplant Vicar of Peter as a claim unique to the papacy. The assertion of the title by the papacy seems originally to have been as much pragmatic in intention as theological in concept. The term Vicar of Christ enabled the pope's name to appear before that of emperors and kings in order of dignity; also, it precluded other bishops from addressing the pope as "brother," as if bishop and pope were on the one level of dignity.

It was Pope Innocent III (1198-1216) who vivified the claim Vicar of Christ for the papacy, writing to the ambassadors of King Philip Augustus of France: "To princes power is given on earth, but to priests it is attributed also in Heaven; to the former only over bodies, to the latter also over souls. Whence it follows that by so much as the soul is superior to the body, the priesthood is superior to the kingship . . . Single rulers have single provinces, and single kings single kingdoms; but Peter, as in the plenitude, so in the extent of his power is preeminent over all, since he is the Vicar of Him whose is the earth and the fullness thereof, the whole wide world and all that dwell therein."

In the title Vicar of Christ rested the authority for Innocent to lay claim to rule the world as a surrogate or Vicar of God. Thus he would write to the Patriarch of Constantinople: "The Lord left to Peter the governance not of the church only, but of the whole world." And to King John of England he would say: "The King of Kings . . . so established the kingship and the priesthood in the church, that the kingship should be priestly, and the priesthood royal, as is evident from the epistle of Peter and the law of Moses, setting one over all, whom he appointed his vicar on earth."

Facts, Myths and Maybes

Lest anyone mistake the seriousness of papal intention, the alternative term Vicar of Peter was not just dropped; it was forbidden. The term Vicar of Peter survived, however, though only marginally. Vicar of Christ became standard terminology. The Jesuit theologian, Saint Robert Bellarmine (1542-1621), embedded Innocent's ideas of Christological vicarship in neo-Scholastic theology, where, stripped of its secular-governance connotations, it has dominated Catholic teaching since as the term expressive of the pope's supreme headship of the church of Christ on earth. In traditional Catholic interpretation of scripture, it is a rank the pope bears by virtue of commission from Christ (Matthew 17:18-19, ''And I say unto thee, that thou art Peter, and upon this rock I shall build my church,'' etc.), and with full vicarial power derived from Christ.

A few theologians have called for a reexamination and qualification of the title Vicar of Christ, again because of the danger of religious exaggeration. Father Richard P. McBrien, for one, has written that ''Vicar of Christ must always be understood in the light of the more traditional title Vicar of Peter. The pope is vicar of Christ because he is a bishop among bishops. He is Vicar of Peter because he is the Bishop of Rome.''

* * *

51

John Deedy

From the vantage point of ecumenical relations, papal infalli-
bility is the church's "bete noir," its black beast.

PERHAPS . . . The doctrine of papal infallibility—
namely, the teaching that the pope cannot err when,
in the authority of office, he speaks on faith and
morals—does indeed belong to a more presumptive
Catholic era.

On the other hand, papal infallibility has been explicitly invoked but once since being written into the
books in 1870 at Vatican Council I. That invoking was
by Pope Pius XII in 1950, when, of course, he declared
the Assumption of Mary into heaven as church dogma.
As noted, the dogma of the Immaculate Conception
was declared by Pius IX in 1854, well before Vatican
I and the official declaration of infallibility. So it's not
as if since 1870 popes have been running about
"infallible-izing" everything in sight. Still, the infallibility decree is fact; it exists, and infallibility accordingly is regarded by some as an ecumenical road block;
it does present a problem for many Protestants.

It might be added that infallibility presents a problem
for some Catholics as well. One recalls, for instance,
the controversy generated by Father Hans Küng's 1971
book *Infallibility? An Inquiry,* in which it was argued
that infallibility belongs only to God and that the
church's legitimate spiritual claim was rather to
"indefectibility or perpetuity in the truth." What that

meant, Küng explained, was that "the church remains in the truth and this is not annulled by the sum total of individual errors." In other words, the church can and does err through the pope—e.g., on Galileo and whether the sun or the earth was the center of the universe; on the sinfulness of charging interest on loans of money; on the separation of church and state, a concept, as noted, once held to be anathema. Notwithstanding, the church remains the community of the faithful, assured of surviving all upheavals; the message of Christ will endure, and Christ will remain "with her in the Spirit and thus keep her through all errors and confusions in the truth."

Küng's proposition seemed innocent enough on the surface, but Rome didn't buy into it. One would have expected as much, for not only would papal authority be diminished by the Küng concept, but also huge chunks of Catholic doctrine would be opened up for re-evaluation, including the Assumption and the Immaculate Conception. So ultimately what happened? Under Roman pressure, Küng's Catholic credentials as a professor at the University of Tubingen in Germany were lifted, and that pretty much settled debate about infallibility versus indefectibility.

So *bete noir* or not, papal infallibility remains a Catholic precept. But, again, the doctrine is not flaunted. In fact, when the one hundredth anniversary of promulgation of the doctrine rolled around in 1970,

Rome let the anniversary pass without official notice. The bypassing of the centenary could have been an ecumenical gesture, or, coming as it did within the time frame of the Küng controversy, it could have reflected sensitivity within the papal household that there was not the meeting of minds on infallibility that there had been hitherto. Whatever the reason, the anniversary quietly passed. But infallibility stays—not exactly the treasure that it was in the age of triumphalism, but official doctrine nonetheless.

*   *   *

There is another form of infallibility besides papal infallibility.

TRUE . . . Ecumenical councils—general assemblies of the world's bishops—are considered infallible, being regarded as the mind of the church in action, the *sensus ecclesiae* taking form and shape through discussion and deliberation, conclusions being set in place through promulgation of dogmatic definitions and decrees, which are then binding on the church.

Technically, only a pope can convoke a council, and only a pope or his legate may preside over the assembly. But this was not always the case. For instance, the Council of Nicaea (325) was called by Constantine the Great, emperor; Constantinople I (381) was brought together jointly by Pope Damasus I and Emperor The-

Facts, Myths and Maybes

odosius I; Nicaea II (787) was convoked by Emperor Constantine VI and his mother, Empress Irene; Constantinople IV (869-870) was summoned by Emperor Basil; Lateran II (1139) met under the impetus of Emperor Conrad. There are other such examples.

Emperors were intimately involved in early councils partly because they held themselves to be guardians or defenders of the faith, and partly in the interests of peace and harmony; large political and social stakes hinged on how religious controversies were settled. Also emperors owned the hall, so to speak. They had the ways and means for facilitating a large gathering of prelates from the far corners of the then-known world. Those days are gone, however. Ecumenical councils are now ecclesiastical assemblies from start to finish.

Further, if a pope dies during an ecumenical council, as happened in the instance of John XXIII and Vatican II, the council is automatically suspended pending a decision by the new pope on whether to proceed or not. Paul VI, of course, elected to continue Vatican II.

* * *

Ecumenical or general councils are decisive moments in ecclesiastical history, as Vatican II demonstrates, and twenty-one of them have been held.

John Deedy

TRUE . . . but only by Rome's count. In the view of some Christian communities, there's been no ecumenical or general council since the beginnings of the schism between East and West. That would make the Second Council of Nicaea in 787 the last truly ecumenical or general council. It was the seventh such assembly.

Strictly speaking, all fourteen councils held since Nicaea II have been papal councils, in the sense that they were convoked or consented to by the pope and have officially involved only those ecclesial communities accepting papal primacy. All fourteen of these councils have been boycotted by the Orthodox Churches of the East, which of course considers Rome in schism from it, hence the East's claim of orthodoxy.

Indeed, it was not until the sixteenth century that Rome itself agreed on the count of ecumenical councils. Confusion arose because some of the general councils of the Middle Ages grew out of synods—convocations of lesser status involving, at least in their beginnings, limited numbers of participants. There was, for instance, uncertainty for a long time about Lateran I and II, held in 1123 and 1139, respectively, and about the Council of Basle, 1433-1437. Lateran I and II were accepted by historians as legitimate councils, but Basle was rejected, for obvious reasons. Basle was largely a council of proxies and doctors that made the mistake of proclaiming as an article of faith its authority over the pope, Eugene IV, thus inviting papal wrath and deposition on charges of heresy.

It was the Jesuit scholar and apologist, Saint Robert Bellarmine, who effectively settled the question of the number of ecumenical or general councils with the enumeration that is accepted today. But, again, that wasn't until the sixteenth century. Bellarmine lived from 1542-1621.

* * *

As pronouncements of the magisterium or teaching church, papal encyclicals are unqualifiedly binding upon Catholics.

FALSE . . . It is agreed that encyclicals are documents of weighty importance. They are not *ex cathedra* or infallible pronouncements however, and fall into a different category from definitions of doctrine concerning faith or morals. Encyclicals are commonly cited by polemicists as clinching details in matters of social, doctrinal or theological dispute. The fact is that whatever the area of discussion, the binding force of encyclicals is itself one of dispute.

In 1950, Pope Pius XII strongly claimed a binding authority for encyclicals, writing in *Humani Generis:* ''Nor must it be thought that what is contained in encyclical letters does not of itself demand assent, on the pretext that the popes do not exercise in them the supreme power of their teaching authority. Rather, such teachings belong to the ordinary magisterium, of which it is true to say: 'He who hears you, hears me' '' (Luke 10:16); for the most part, too, what is expounded and inculcated in encyclical letters already appertains to Catholic doctrine for other reasons. But if the supreme pontiffs in their official documents purposely pass judgment on a matter debated until then, it is obvious to all that the matter, according to the mind and will of the same pontiffs, cannot be considered any longer a question open for discussion among theologians.''

On the other hand, the 1913 *Catholic Encyclopedia* (The Gilmary Society, New York) states: ''The degree to which the infallible magisterium of the Holy See is committed [in an encyclical] must be judged from the circumstances, and from the language used in the particular case.''

The two sources make points directly opposite to one another.

One encounters a similar dichotomy in Catholic tradition on the subject, persons virtually in the one breath minimizing, then maximizing what binds the Catholic conscience. For instance, some will insist on the binding nature of Paul VI's birth control encyclical, *Humanae Vitae;* then they'll dismiss as academic Protestant objection to the doctrine of infallibility, noting it has been invoked but once since its definition in 1870. Well, are popes regularly binding Catholic consciences through the issuance of encyclicals, or are they rarely doing so because the invocation of infallibility is rare? One can't have it both ways.

The bottom line is that encyclicals per se are not *ex cathedra* documents invested with the infallible authority of the promulgating pope; they are not statements binding in faith or morals, as in the case of the doctrine of the Assumption infallibly pronounced by Pius XII in 1950. Rather, an encyclical is a weighty document expressing the mind of the church as reflected in the thinking of the reigning pontiff, but the contents do not become dogma by fact of being included in an encyclical.

In point of fact, to hark back for a minute to infallibility, it is not exactly easy for a pope to speak infallibly. Several conditions must be met. First, he must pronounce himself on a matter of faith or morals; then he must speak as the Vicar of Christ, in his office of pope, and to the church universal; finally, and most important, he must make clear his intention to speak *ex cathedra* ("from the chair" of Peter), as with the use of such a term as "we/I proclaim," "we/I define," etc. Furthermore, infallibility belongs strictly speaking only to that portion of the document or pronouncement which is specified as such. For instance, the 1854 bull proclaiming the Immaculate Conception doctrine, *Ineffabilis Deus,* was quite long, but only those few sentences pronouncing and defining Mary's exemp-

tion from Original Sin are construed as being infallible. The rest is open to the same judgment as came
to be rendered on Pope Benedict XIV's *Vix Pervenit*
restating condemnation of interest charges on finan-
cial loans. It was rejected as morally naive and
economically impractical.

* * *

*Modern-day dissenters from church teaching are, in effect,
latter-day Donatists.*

DEBATABLE . . . Professor Emeritus Samuel Terrien
of Union Theological Seminary argues they are, in an
essay on Graham Greene in *Theology Today* for January
1992, saying "in modern usage" the term applies
loosely to "Roman Catholics who question the pronouncements of the hierarchy in their struggle to
understand the profundity and the demands of the
Gospels."

But are today's questioners and dissenters in fact
Donatists?

First, about the label. It derives from a fourth-century
North African bishop named Donatus and a sect that
refused to separate the validity of the sacraments from
the moral character of the administering priest. In other
words, the validity and efficacy of all sacerdotal acts
depended upon the personal character of the administrator. If the administrator was not personally in a state

of grace, the sacerdotal act was invalid. It followed that a church that tolerated unworthy administrators lost the vital attributes of purity and catholicity. The task, accordingly, was to protect the church's holiness by excluding those officials who had committed serious or mortal sin, as well as those who received their authority or ecclesial status from those officials. They were to be anathematized, read out of the church—or worse.

There seems a double problem in applying the term Donatists to today's church.

On the one hand, the dissenters Professor Terrien alludes to—namely, the Graham Greenes of our times, not the Archbishop Lefebvres—are not anathematizing or excommunicating anyone. By and large, these are people who regard the church in pluralistic ways, with plenty of room for dissenters. The reaction to *Humanae Vitae*, the 1968 birth-control encyclical, is a case in point. The clamor of the dissenters from the encyclical was loud, but they did not appropriate orthodoxy to themselves, as might the Donatists of old, nor did they quit the church; they stayed and made their decision-making a matter for their individual consciences.

On the other hand, neither is the church itself acting Donatist and anathematizing dissenters from doctrine or questioners of official pronouncement the way it once did. For instance, since the 1983 revision of the

John Deedy

Code of Canon Law, a validly married Catholic who divorces and remarries is no longer excommunicated. That person may no longer participate in the sacramental life of the church, but the person remains a part of the church.

Strange as it may seem, the confronting of the Donatist controversy at the Council of Arles in 314 and again at the Council of Carthage in 411 may in the long run have had something to do with this mutual tolerance.

In condemning Donatism, the early church fathers declared that sacerdotal acts, specifically the administration of the sacraments, derived their efficacy from Christ, and not from the spiritual state or condition of their human administrators. By the same token, the church's holiness . . . better, its purity and catholicity were not vitiated by the presence in it of persons who were not "worthy members" in the traditional sense of the term. Ours, in a word, is a human church. Thus, ordination at the hands of a personally unworthy cleric is still a valid ordination; a properly administered baptism, whether by unworthy individual or indeed by a heretic, is still a valid sacrament.

If the church's purity and catholicity were not impugned by unworthy ministers of the sacraments, how can it be by the presence of those "who question the pronouncements of the hierarchy"?

So who then are today's Donatists?

Facts, Myths and Maybes

They don't appear to be the dissenters. Nor the hierarchs. The term just doesn't apply.

* * *

Because of Mary's exalted position in the church, Marian messages, such as those of Lourdes and Fatima, are of special importance and binding on Catholics.

MYTH . . . Marian messages arrive through Marian apparitions, so-called, and belong to what is known as private revelation; that is, revelation for the benefit of one individual or group of individuals. Private revelation is not intended for all the faithful or all of history; for instance, private revelation is not accompanied by any divine guarantee, such as with the deposit of the faith entrusted by God to the church, that it will be transmitted without adulteration. Said another way, however weighty the church's approbation of a particular apparition and its message, there is no guarantee of authenticity.

Church approbation then of a particular private revelation and its message merely connotes permission, extended after due examination, to publicize the revelation and message for the edification and utility of believers. Private revelation does not pass into the deposit of faith; it is not subsumed into the truth which God committed to the church; it does not become dogmatic teaching.

John Deedy

Thus, so far as the apparitions of Lourdes and Fatima are concerned, one is free to believe or disbelieve, heed the messages or dismiss them as fanciful. The same goes for Medjugore, and all the rest.

Theories exist that private revelation or apparitions belong to cycles of church history, Marian apparitions no less than any other.

Apropos Marian apparitions, they came to multiply after apparitions in other devotional areas—e.g., to Saint Catherine of Genoa on purgatory; to Saint Margaret Mary Alacoque on devotion to the Sacred Heart—had run their course, and a void suddenly existed in then-traditional Catholicism. Coincidental or not, the multiplication of Marian messages was rapid. To cite the more famous Marian apparitions, there was LaSalette in 1846, Lourdes in 1858, Knock in 1879, Fatima in 1917. In fact, from mid-nineteenth century until mid-twentieth century, the church was in what might be called a ''Marian age,'' one that peaked with Pius XII's consecration of the entire human race to the Immaculate Heart of Mary in 1942 (under the influence of Fatima, it is said), his establishment of the Feast of the Queenship of Mary in 1945, and, most dramatically, his promulgation of the dogma of the Assumption in 1950.

Since cycles are of limited duration, has the Marian cycle too run its course?

Facts, Myths and Maybes

Some think so, and trace the cause to Vatican Council II. Vatican II, it will be recalled, criticized the excesses of Marianism ("Let the faithful remember moreover that true devotion [to the Blessed Mary] consists neither in a fruitless and passing emotion, nor in a vain credulity," *Lumen gentium,* 67), and of course Vatican II declined to build on Marian dogma by declaring Mary mediatrix or co-redemptrix of humankind with her son, despite enormous pressure to do so. Whether there's a subtle relationship between what happened at the Council and the present eclipse of Marian devotion is anyone's guess; likely much more is involved than what happened at the Council alone. All that is certain is that the eclipse is very real.

There's Medjugore, of course, and the Marian apparitions that are alleged to have begun there in 1981. However, one is cautious in their regard. The principal prelate of the area for one, Bishop Pavao Zanic of Mostar-Duvno, has dismissed them as "collective hallucination."

* * *

In Catholic consciousness, the seven sacraments are the church's channels of grace, the signs which proclaim faith.

FACT . . . By catechical definition, the sacraments are outward signs instituted by Jesus Christ to bring grace

John Deedy

to souls. In conciliar understanding, they are acts of the church that give expression to the church's nature and its mission. There are seven sacraments: baptism, Holy Eucharist, confirmation, reconciliation (penance), matrimony, anointing of the sick (extreme unction), and Holy Orders (diaconate and priesthood). Three of them—baptism, confirmation and Holy Orders—can be received only once, as they produce a permanent effect in the recipient; old catechisms called this an "indelible mark," a "sacramental character" that is never lost. The four other sacraments may be received as often as preference and conditions of eligibility are met— e.g., Communion may be received daily by persons in a state of grace, and on given occasions more than once a day; similarly, a married man or woman is free to remarry sacramentally on the death of a spouse.

All seven sacraments have specific purposes and effects. What they have in common is that they are external signs of something sacred. Theirs is a commonality presumptive from the very definition of the word sacrament. Sacrament is from the Latin *sacramentum*, which signifies an external thing endowed with a meaning and purpose beyond itself. In Roman law, that thing was the money, *sacramentum,* deposited by litigants to a suit as a kind of escrow fund; in the Roman military, it was the oath of fidelity soldiers took pledging not to desert or abandon their responsibilities. Christians gave the word its religious understanding by applying it to sacred rites, then particularized it in terms of the seven sacraments.

*   *   *

The number of sacraments was not fixed at seven until the twelfth century.

FACT . . . Until the twelfth century the number of sacraments ranged from twelve to as many as thirty, depending upon the source. How come? For centuries all signs of sacred things were broadly called sacraments, so naturally there was great confusion between a sacrament in the general sense and a sacrament in the particular sense.

The matter began to sort itself out in the ninth century, but it was not until the French philosopher and theologian Peter Abelard (the same of the Heloise and Abelard legend) produced his roll of six sacraments early in the twelfth century that the issue was close to resolution. Abelard listed baptism, confirmation, Holy Eucharist, penance, matrimony and extreme unction as sacraments in the strict and formal sense, but not Holy Orders—an omission which probably spoke more about his passion for Heloise than his theology.

It was Peter Lombard (c1100-1160), an Italian theologian who spent most of his life in France, who finally defined the number of sacraments as seven, fitting each within a systematized theology built on an understanding of signs of grace. This was in his fourth *Book of Sentences*. Christian history then stood at about the year 1150.

The Second Council of Lyons (1274) confirmed Peter Lombard's enumeration, and its action has been accepted since throughout Catholicism.

* * *

Sacramentals may be said to be "little sacraments."

MAYBE . . . Certainly the word suggests as much, being so close etymologically to sacrament. And indeed the term did come into common use with the refinement of what was a sacrament and what was not. Which takes one back again to the previous item and the twelfth and thirteenth centuries.

Sacramentals complemented sacraments. That was the theologians' conclusion, and they arrived at it by determining whether a rite or ritual produced grace *ex opere operanto* or not—that is, whether it effected grace by virtue of its administration, and not solely through faith in divine promises or the merit and disposition of the user (*ex opere operantis*).

By theological definition, sacraments communicated grace *ex opere operanto,* by virtue of its administration. Sacramentals, on the other hand, communicated grace *quasi ex opere operanto*—that is, in a way resembling the sacraments, but not automatically so by virtue of the rite or substance employed. Peter Lombard explained it all in *Sentences*.

Sacramentals, then, are piously said to be favors from God conveyed through the church forgiving minor sins, remitting temporal punishment due to sin, conveying bodily health, material blessings, protection from evil spirits, etc. Hence the use of relics, medals, statues, holy candles, etc., as objects of special holiness by reason of association or the items' being blessed.

But mostly, as mentioned, sacramentals complement sacraments. Thus, for example, the use of holy water is connected to baptism; the distribution of ashes on Ash Wednesday is connected to penance (reconciliation); the blessing of homes and various blessings of women are connected to matrimony; sick bed and burial rites are connected to extreme unction (sacrament of the sick).

The bottom line is that most everything blessed qualifies as being ''in the service of the sacraments,'' and is therefore a sacramental.

* * *

Matrimony is a sacrament of the laity.

LITERALLY and FIGURATIVELY . . . and not only because of the exclusion of priests from marrying under present church discipline. Marriage is a sacrament of the laity because the contracting couple not only marry one another, but because the marrying woman and man are the actual ministers of the sacrament. They marry one another in biological and sacramental fact. The priest is present not as "marrier," but as a witness on behalf of the church—and additionally the state, of course, the priest's being licensed accordingly.

All this is consistent with historical tradition. Matrimony was an established social institution long before Christendom, and apart from tightening the reins over divorce and stressing the responsibilities of the partners within marriage, Christ did not seek to remake it as social or religious contract. The state regulated marriage, and that was acceptable. The church was three to four centuries old before it moved to regulate and control marriage, certainly in the instance of the baptized.

Two factors contributed to change bringing the priest (or permanent deacon in the new order of things) into the marriage ceremony as major player. One was the increasing practice on the part of married couples to ask the blessing of the church on their union; a second was to curb abuses of marriage as a sacrament by having present an official witness to the ceremony. Generally, the church (the state, as well) had been content so long as marriages were contracted publicly. But the private or secret marriage presented problems, since they could be easily concealed or denied, thus complicating inheritances and fostering bigamy. Enter the priest as official witness to marriage.

But for Mr. & Mrs. Doe, the priest's presence doesn't change the answer to the question, "Who married you?" It wasn't Father; it was the Does themselves.

* * *

Confirmation is the problem sacrament in the lexicon of sacramental rites.

TRUE . . . The historical reality is that confirmation did not exist as a separate sacramental rite until the third century. The very term confirmation was not used until the French Councils of Riez and Orange in 439 and 441, and the confirmation rite itself was not a common one until after the fifth century.

In fact, well into the Middle Ages theologians were arguing about the origin of confirmation. Hugh of St. Victor and Peter Lombard held that confirmation was instituted by the Holy Spirit through the instrument of the Apostles; the Dominican position was that Christ himself was the immediate author of the sacrament; Franciscan theory was that the Holy Spirit instituted the sacrament acting through the Apostles or through the church after the death of the Apostles. There was less debate in the churches of the Reformation; they jettisoned confirmation as a sacrament, a few retain-

71

ing bare elements of the rite for pastoral purposes.

Confirmation's problem is rooted in the fact that there is no precise scriptural documentation for it as sacrament, though some see its institution in Christ's promise to send the Paraclete. The authenticity problem is compounded by the shaky nature of key documents providing it with a provenance or sacramental lineage; as Joseph Martos notes in *Doors to the Sacred* (Doubleday, 1982), these documents proved to be ninth-century French forgeries devised to protect French clerical prerogatives against claims of emperor and nobles.

The Second Council of Lyons in 1274 nonetheless listed confirmation among the seven sacraments of the church. Later councils were less dogmatic, however. The Council of Trent (1545-1563) held confirmation to be a sacrament and anathematized those who viewed it a useless ceremony, but otherwise it gave the subject of confirmation perfunctory treatment. Not needing to be specific, Vatican Council II (1962-1965) was ambiguous. Its references to confirmation were brief, and framed in the context of the Holy Spirit and confirmation's link to baptism.

The baptismal association long was important, for it was baptism that initially furnished confirmation its liturgical *raison d'etre*. The two were administered in the one ceremony, a practice still followed in Eastern Orthodoxy. The liturgical rationale grew that confirmation made fast—*confirmed*, as it were—the sacramental sign of baptism, while adding a sacramental dimension making the individual a perfect Christian . . . or as used to be said before the shedding of militaristic images, a "soldier of Jesus Christ."

It is easy to understand how confirmation would come to be regarded as a sacrament. In the early church, baptisms were performed by bishops, and the ceremony concluded with an anointing and imposition of the bishop's hand. This many saw as a receiving of the seven gifts of the Holy Spirit (wisdom, understanding, counsel, fortitude, knowledge, piety and fear of the Lord).

As Christianity grew and baptisms multiplied enormously, baptism became less and less an episcopal rite, and one that was instead presided over by a priest. For a time it was common to take the newly baptized person to a bishop for the postbaptismal anointing and imposition of hands that theoretically completed and sealed the sacrament of baptism. But this practice ended, as much for reasons of logistics as anything else. It was not exactly easy to travel about pre-Henry Ford.

The rites of baptism and confirmation were thus separated, and the separation did nothing for confirmation's popularity. The rite fell into disuse, to such an extent that sanctions as serious as excommunication were threatened against those neglecting its existence. Not surprisingly, the mandates of observance

John Deedy

and respect often were honored indifferently; instances were known, for example, of the sacrament being administered by a bishop passing through a town on horseback, reaching out and anointing as he rode by.

Matters are not that casual today. Nonetheless, confirmation continues to be a problem for some sacramental theologians. They see confirmation as sign, but at the same time many are hard pressed to see it also as cause of grace—an essential element in the definition of a sacrament as an outward sign instituted by God/Christ to give grace. For many of the latter the sacrament reduces to a kind of ecclesiastical equivalent of initiation into a secret society or elite group. Even so, confirmation is accounted an experience of the Holy Spirit, and as such remains an important religious rite.

* * *

On the other hand, in terms of Catholic practice and observance, penance or reconciliation is the real problem sacramental rite.

TRUE . . . and many find this difficult to understand. For one thing, no one Catholic sacrament is so scripturally documented as penance, or as the sacrament is known now, reconciliation; to wit: John 20:22-23, "Whose sins you shall forgive . . . etc."; Matthew 16:19, "Whatsoever you shall bind on earth . . . etc."; Acts 19:18, "Many who had become believers came

forward and openly confessed their former practices.''
In the days of contented flocks, flourishing schools and
crowded church parking lots on Sunday mornings—
which wasn't so long ago, really—there was no surer
mark of American Catholicism than the Saturday after-
noon and evening confessional line. Everyone, it
seemed, went to confession at least once a month. Now
no one goes.

Well, not quite no one. A 1983 University of Notre
Dame survey of 2,667 non-Hispanic American Catholics with ties to parishes showed that it was only 26
percent who never went to confession at all. But—and
this is a large *but*—only 6 percent confessed once a
month, and only 1 percent more often than that. For
all practical purposes, the sacrament of penance or
reconciliation has been mothballed by American
Catholics. And no one knows for sure why.

The more gloomy regard the drop-off in sacramental confessions as another reflection of the so-called loss
or diminishment of a sense of sin in the new generations of Catholics to the cultural and secular forces
around them. Others attribute it to an ability to experience forgiveness and reconciliation through better,
more agreeable methods. For instance, as in Protestantism, many Catholics apparently have come to feel
that they are their own best mediators before God.
What need then for a priest except in extraordinary instances? Finally, frequent communion may account for

at least some of the change. The dullest student of the old Baltimore Catechism knows that venial sins need not be confessed, that they are remitted by good works, prayer, contrition and "fervent communion." Under such a logic, might not communion then be for some a form of confession?

Whatever the explanation(s) for the eclipse of the sacrament, it is erroneous to believe that the problem just snuck up on the church. The *New York Times* suggested as much in 1990, remarking that the matter of frequent confession "did not figure in the documents of the Second Vatican Council . . . or in the monumental debates surrounding the Council." Yet the Council Fathers must have been aware that something was amiss and needed attention, for in *Sacrosanctum Concilium*, the Constitution on the Sacred Liturgy, they counseled that "the rite and formulas for the sacrament of penance are to be revised so that they give more luminous expression to both the nature and effect of the sacrament" (72).

The revision ordered by the Council was promulgated by the Vatican's Congregation for Divine Worship in 1974. Among other things, it restated standard doctrine concerning the sacrament, reemphasized the social (communal and ecclesial) aspects of sin, and prescribed new forms for celebration and reception of the sacrament, without doing away with the old. Among the new options were face-to-face confession,

Facts, Myths and Maybes

rather than from behind a screen, and a communal penitential rite, followed by individual confession. None has turned the situation around. For better or for worse, the sacrament of penance, reconciliation, continues to founder on the rocks of indifference.

What reading should one put on that? The doom-sayers no doubt regard the phenomenon as further evidence of the domino effects of a Council that went too far. The more optimistic may see it as development of doctrinal practice, or the working of what Newman might have called *sensus fidelium,* the sense of the faithful. In a word, change at the grassroots.

* * *

Controversy involving confession, First Communion and the Catholic child is theologically akin to the chicken-and-the-egg riddle. Re. the chicken and the egg: Which came first? Re. confession, First Communion and the child: Which should come first?

INDEED . . . there is controversy about when a child should begin confessing, and the controversy is rooted in the theology of the Eucharist.

Eucharistic theology calls for one to be in the state of grace in order to receive communion "worthily"; that is, one must be free of grave or serious sin—mortal sin, if you will. In the context of First Communion, is a child 7-years-old (normal age for reception of First

Communion) capable of grave or serious sin? If not, what need of confessing (reconciling, in new terminology) before First Communion? Does the practice not confuse the child and at the same time trivialize the sacrament of reconciliation?

But maybe, one objects, the child has committed venial sin (though that too's a behavioral question mark for one who's just reaching the age of reason). In any instance, no problem. Venial sin is not an impediment to ''worthy'' reception of communion—First Communion or, for that matter, second, third, fourth, forty-fourth, whenever. Communion, in fact, remits venial sin—wipes it out. So again, why disturb the child's psyche and layer innocence with notions of sin, especially at such a beautiful time as First Communion? Wouldn't it be better to delay First Confession, exalt First Communion, and use the separation time to make clearer the distinctive nature of the two sacraments?

These were points of great issue in the years after Vatican II (1962-1965), as theologians were examining norms of the sacraments. Pope Saint Pius X (1903-1914) had joined First Confession and First Communion in 1910 with the decree *Quam singulari*. After the council, however, a number of dioceses began experimenting with two- and three-year programs deferring reception of First Confession. The experimentations were especially widespread in the U.S., with more than half the dioceses adopting policies of separation and deferral.

After initially approving the experimentation, Rome reversed ground. On May 24, 1973, the Congregation for the Discipline of the Sacraments and the Congregation for the Clergy together issued *Sanctus Pontifex*, a decree ordering the termination of all programs of separation by the end of the following school year. The decree held that devotional reception of penance was as valid for children as for adults, and said sound catechetical instruction would take care of any confusions that might arise about the distinct and separate nature of the two sacraments.

Surprisingly, many dioceses ignored the instruction—so many, in fact, that in 1977 the Vatican congregations reiterated the order of four years before: "... All experimentations of receiving First Communion without the sacrament of penance should cease, so that the discipline of the church might be restored in the spirit of the decree *Quam singulari*."

Uniformity of practice did not result, however. Some dioceses continue to have separate programs of preparation for the two sacraments; others conduct simultaneous programs of preparation, then offer children (and their parents) the option of receiving the sacraments together or receiving communion now, penance later. The policies are based on traditional eucharistic theology: a person free of serious sin cannot be "re-quired" to confess before receiving communion, even for First Communion. It is also contended that Rome's instructions are disciplinary, not doctrinal, and there-fore are subject to the interpretation of the local bishop.

On the other hand, Canon 914 of the code of Canon Law states confession should precede First Com-munion.

* * *

Justification by faith is a fundamental Catholic principle.

WRONG . . . Justification by faith is often designated the "material principle" of Lutheranism and, through Lutheranism, of Protestantism generally. As such, it is the classical formulation of a central Protestant principle.

By definition, justification is the act by which God makes a person just, and the consequent change in the spiritual status of that person from sin to grace. For Catholics this transformation involves good works; for Protestants it involves faith alone.

While Protestants have widely different views on the matter of Original Sin many hold that through the fall of Adam, human nature became evil. Christ's death atoned for evil, but evil remains. In humankind it is redeemed not by works, but by confidence that the merits of Christ are actually applied to us. These merits cover, as it were, our sins and imperfections. Sin, in other words, is not imputed to us by God, but the merits of Christ are. The act of faith, which confesses Christ as savior, is the only act needed for justification.

This Protestant doctrine is rooted in Martin Luther's fundamental insistence that there must be a death of self and a new birth of Christ. Once this occurs, good works are of no necessary avail for justification; they're actually unnecessary, since the merits of Christ have been applied to us. Repentance then consists in a change of the moral attitude of mind and soul, with divine forgiveness following—again without need of reparation or works.

However, to believe that grace is an offering of God, which is not dependent upon people's good works, is not to say that works of love are irrelevant for Protestants. Most Protestants would sense that the Epistle of James, which stresses action as a result of faith (2:14-26), counterbalances Paul's Letter to the Romans, the biblical source of the concept of faith as God-given grace (3:25; 5:1). Doing good is a natural result of receiving grace.

Catholic teaching on justification is the opposite of Protestantism's.

As expounded by the Council of Trent (1545-1563) over sixteen chapters and thirty-three canons, Catholic teaching links justification with the sacraments, beginning with baptism (which frees the recipient from sin,

John Deedy

original and personal) and continuing most notably through the sacrament of penance or reconciliation, with its essential elements of contrition, confession and satisfaction (works). For Catholics, justification then is the process by which the soul is regenerated by grace. It is merited by Christ's death on the cross. Though God, of course, works in the soul, the individual's part and the role of faith are indispensable.

Said another way, Catholic teaching holds that faith alone cannot justify the individual. Since our relationship with God is based on perfect love of God and charity, faith devoid of charity and good works possesses no justifying power. Once justified in the soul by God, however, the individual can grow (increase) in holiness and grace by good works and the meriting of indulgences.

Additional factors differentiate Protestant and Catholic understandings of justification. For Protestants, the qualities of justification are certainty, equality and permanency; it is impossible ever to lose it. For Catholics, the qualities of justification are uncertainty, inequality and amissibility. It can be blotted out; it can be lost.

* * *

Predestination, a principle commonly identified with John Calvin and other Protestants, presents no particular problem in Catholic theology.

Facts, Myths and Maybes

WRONG, AGAIN . . . Catholic theology rejects absolute predestination as vitiating God's divine justice, as well as of the principle of free will. Still, predestination is a teaching not easily dealt with, nor totally dismissible.

In essence, predestination is the doctrine that God in his infallible prescience of the future knows all events and deeds occurring in time, and further, has eternally chosen or destined those who will be saved and those who will not. In effect, then, he preordains the good or evil that people will do, and therefore whether they will be saved or damned. As taught by John Calvin, French leader of the Reformation in Switzerland, there is certitude of salvation for the elect, and the elect are incapable of losing grace. As with the topic of justification by faith, the principal biblical source is Paul's Epistle to the Romans: ''For whom he did foreknow, he also did predestinate to be conformed to the image of his son, that he might be the firstborn among many brethren. Moreover whom he did predestinate, them he also called; and whom he called, them he also justified; and whom he justified, them he also glorified'' (Romans 8:29-30).

Catholic teaching differentiates between potency and act, and holds that while a person's salvation is completely in the hands of God, it is also in his or her own hands. Eternally, God has prepared the gifts of grace to call persons to salvation, and to assist them in times of temptation and trial, while at the same time providing individuals the virtues by which they may merit salvation. Some will respond positively, others will not. Those responding to God's call receive God's gift. What of the others? Their failure is held to be their own, for of their own free will they rejected God's will for their salvation.

But does not Catholic teaching put some people at an advantage in gaining salvation, and others at a disadvantage? Are not the people of Catholic Ireland, say, better situated to receive and maximize the gifts of grace than those of Ethiopia or some other country, where the populace is largely unbaptized and efficacious graces largely unknown—where, for instance, survival, not salvation, is the operative force in human existence? To many in Ethiopia a loaf of bread is of infinitely more worth and importance than a novena of Masses or the opportunity to gain graces by making a retreat.

The objection is one of long standing, for the unequal distribution of baptismal and other graces in the world has forever troubled Catholic theologians. Why should people in one part of the world know the God of Christianity so well, and be privy to that God's blessings, and people of other lands, or next door for that matter, experience little or nothing from that same God? How could prescient God drown an Ireland in baptismal waters, and leave an Ethiopia to misery and a missionary fate?

These are hard questions.

Still, the church holds that although God has a real will for the salvation of all peoples, he definitely chooses some for eternal life, and leaves others out of that choice. Scripturally it has no choice, for there's Mark 13:22: "[They] shall show signs and wonders, to seduce, if it were possible, even the elect"; and there's Matthew 24:31, "They shall gather together his elect from the four winds," etc. Isn't this predestination? Certainly seems so. But how does one account for such a God of preference?

Augustine's answer, delivered in the earliest days of the debate, was: *Inscrutabilia sunt judicia Dei*, "the judgments of God are inscrutable."

In the Middle Ages and later, Aquinas and theologians such as Robert Bellarmine and Suarez developed a distinction between efficacious graces for the privileged (the elect), so that during their lifetimes they would correspond with God's impulses, and sufficient graces for the others, so that no one was left out of the divine plan of salvation for all. Appended then was the rationale of predestination *ante praevisa merita* (predestination antecedent to the prevision of merit); that is, the choice of the elect resulted as an act of pure benevolence on God's part and not because of their foreseen merits.

Not everyone signed on to those opinions. In fact, some theologians argued the opposite, contending that the Thomist proposition led inexorably to Calvinist doctrine of absolute predestination.

The differences were never resolved, and the church never ruled. As a 1948 Catholic source book counsels, "In these discussions every Catholic is at liberty to take whichever [Catholic] side he prefers, provided that he is always ready to submit to any decision which the church may make."

Not exactly satisfactory, but then as the Council of Trent said way back in the sixteenth century, predestination is a "hidden mystery."

Apparently it so remains.

*   *   *

In Catholic eschatology, the "four last things" are Death, Judgment, Heaven and Hell.

FACT . . . Eschatology is the branch of systematic theology that deals with the doctrines of last things, and, yes, in Catholic eschatology the "four last things" are Death, Judgment, Heaven and Hell. The enumeration is more popular than scientific, however—and in many of the subdivisions, the details thoroughly problematical. Relatively little has been dogmatically defined regarding the "four last things," and, as will be seen, theologians (as distinct from many preachers and

Facts, Myths and Maybes

popular writers) are cautious in their pronouncements; e.g., on Purgatory and Limbo. The Fathers of Vatican II (1962-1965) openly confessed their limitation of knowledge in *Gaudium et spes,* the Pastoral Constitution on the Church in the Modern World: "We do not know the time for the consumation of the earth and of humanity. Nor do we know how all things will be transformed. As deformed by sin, the shape of this world will pass. But we are taught that God is preparing a new dwelling place and a new earth where justice will abide, and whose blessedness will answer and surpass all the longings for peace which spring up in the human heart" (39).

* * *

Death, which is the separation of the soul from the body, will be followed by Judgment—indeed, two Judgments, one Particular and the other General.

FACT . . . According to broad Catholic theology, a Particular Judgment will follow immediately after death for all individuals, whereupon each will be rewarded or punished according to her or his merits, with the sentence promptly fulfilled. Another General Judgment will occur at the end of the world, in order, as the Catechism tells us, "to show forth God's glory and the glory of the just, and to put the wicked to shame." Theoretically, the General Judgment is to take place in one instance, and through a divine illumination each individual will completely understand her or his own moral condition and that of everyone else's.

Historically, the idea of a Particular Judgment evolved largely from the parable of Dives and Lazarus told in Luke 16:19. Dives is the rich man who does not give the scraps from his table to the poor man, Lazarus, sitting at the gate. When the two finally die, Dives is consigned to Hell, while Lazarus goes to Heaven. There's further support for the teaching in John 5:22, where upon death the individual stands in the presence of God, specifically God the Son, to give an account of life, and thereupon is assigned her or his fate.

The idea of a collective General Judgment is described throughout the Bible, notably in Daniel and the Book of Revelation. In a sense, this General Judgment is a public repetition of Particular Judgments, only now, as said, for the instruction of all and in display of the justice, wisdom and mercy of God.

But this is all old theology. As Passionist Father Donald Senior, professor of New Testament studies at Catholic Theological Union in Chicago, once commented, in *U.S. Catholic*, if the church were to speak to the subject of Last Judgment, there'd be a ''big hesitation'' about moving much beyond traditional thinking. ''There's actually a lot of latitude in official teaching on the Last Judgment,'' he remarked—understandably enough, since the Bible itself is inconclusive on the subject. "The purpose of the Judgment texts in the Scriptures is more one of moral persuasion," Senior noted, including in the New Testament, where "the purpose is to bring the person to conversion." The Old Testament texts are similarly vague. There the emphasis is more on life of earth, and there really isn't a lot of room for details about a Last Judgment.

The Nicene Creed speaks about Christ sitting at the right hand of the Father and coming to judge the living and the dead, and Catholics profess that at every mass they attend. Still, like the Trinity, the Last Judgment, Particular or General, is essentially a mystery.

* * *

Heaven is the natural destiny of all Catholics.

FACT . . . Heaven, indeed, is the natural destiny of all creatures, and according to a *USA Weekend* magazine poll of a few years ago, nearly three-quarters of all Americans (to narrow the focus) believe they have an "excellent" or "good" chance of getting there. The big questions, of course, are where and what is Heaven?

The Catholic answer is that Heaven is a place, although whether with walls massive and high, and with twelve gates at which twelve angels will be stationed, as described by John in chapter 21 of the Book of Revelation (Apocalypse) is doubtful. For all the detail about gleaming radiance and inscriptions commemor-

ating the twelve tribes of Israel, John's must be accounted a figurative or metaphorical description. Still,
Catholic theology says that Heaven is out there somewhere. As one source has it, John's account would be
"altogether deceptive unless Heaven were a place in
some way circumscribed and limited."

As for the "what" of Heaven, traditional Catholic
teaching is that it is a place of perfect bliss and happiness, the essence of which is the sight of God face
to face. This is the Beatific Vision, defined as "the
immediate knowledge of God which constitutes the
primary felicity of Heaven."

Fine, except it is difficult to imagine eternal happiness
and satisfaction consisting of one endless act of contemplation and love. Corot said that he hoped with
all his heart that there will be painting in Heaven. He
had a point. Heaven, it would seem, would become
in time something of a great bore, and God himself
(herself) inevitably would come to appear an unrelieved
egoist, if God were the end all and be all of Heaven.
Imagine anyone, least of all God, expecting billions of
people to spend their eternities basking in his/her vision, however beatific!

Traditional teaching has a double response to that
difficulty. First, the Beatific Vision is classified as a
mystery; the human mind cannot fully fathom it or its
potential for satisfying forever, any more than the
human mind can grasp the Trinity in its totality of

meaning. Second, the Beatific Vision isn't all; there are what are said to be the "secondary sources" of happiness in Heaven: the vision of the incarnate God, Jesus Christ, and the company of Mary, the Angels and the saints. Isn't that enough to make Heaven a place of endless joy and interest? It has even been proposed that in Heaven individuals will discover a special "bond of affection and intimacy" between themselves and their Guardian Angels.

But, of course, all that is speculation. The bottom line is that no one knows what Heaven holds aside from the Beatific Vision. For that matter, no one knows exactly what the Beatific Vision comprises. Father Richard P. McBrien says in *Catholicism* (Winston, 1980), that the Beatific Vision is the "full union of the human person with God. . . . It is the completion of all that we are as human beings . . . the fulfillment of who we are and what we are called to become."

Does that mean that Heaven will be a place devoid of creative restlessness and creative activity? Check with Corot as soon as you get there.

* * *

The Scriptures speak of a multiplicity of Heavens.

FACT . . . and so do others. Scriptural references to a plurality of heavens are contained both in the Old and the New Testaments; e.g., Psalms 148:4, and 2

John Deedy

Timothy 4:6-8. More explicitly, Saint Paul in 2 Corinthians 12:3 speaks of being "snatched up to the third Heaven." In medieval times, the theory of three Heavens was common. Saint Teresa of Avila in one of her mystical experiences mentions being in the lower Heaven. Similarly, the Swedish theologian and mystic Emmanuel Swedenborg espoused a theory of a plurality of Heavens—Hells too, for that matter—probably as many as three of each.

Islam multiplies the possibility. It proposes seven graded Heavens, with individuals going to the level earned on earth. The Seventh Heaven is the one of ineffable bliss—hence the phrase designating ultimate joy, "being in Seventh Heaven." In Islam's Seventh Heaven there are 70,000 tongues that speak 70,000 languages, all endlessly chanting the praises of Allah.

Islam's concept may seem exotic, but the idea of seven Heavens has roots as far back as Babylonian and Sumerian antiquity. Some early fathers of the church even had concepts of a sevenfold division of the heavens, perhaps derivative of Jewish theories of seven concentric revolving spheres of spirits and extraterrestrial beings.

Catholic tradition allows that Heaven will not be the same for all; in other words, the Beatific Vision will be bestowed on those attaining Heaven according to the merit of each. It's like Saint Thomas said in the *Summa Theologica:* "He shares more fully in the light of glory who possesses the greater love . . . he who has more love will see God more perfectly and be more blessed" (1, Q. 12, art. 6). But Catholic tradition is emphatic: there's only one Heaven.

* * *

Hell is sheer hell—a place of unrelieved agony of the mind over the loss of the Beatific Vision, and pain to the senses from the torments of fire.

MAYBE . . . According to traditional Catholic theology, those are indeed the punishments of Hell, and they're supposed to last for all time. There are some difficulties, however.

First the Beatific Vision. In traditional understanding, how effective can its loss be in terms of the damned? As remarked by Rev. J. P. Arendzen in *The Teaching of the Catholic Church* (Macmillan, 1949), the pain of loss depends on a realization of the value of the thing lost. His point: unless the soul of the departed person en route to Hell is granted some greater realization of what God is than what was possessed on earth, the deprivation of the vision of God will mean nothing.

On the other hand, once God is seen face to face, tradition says that vision is never withdrawn from that soul, and it follows that the soul will love God forever.

How then reconcile the two propositions? If the damned person sees God face to face in judgment, does

John Deedy

he or she go to Hell actually loving God? Further, if the damned person takes along a love of God and something of the vision of God, then what's the point of Hell?

Yesterday's theologian suggested that at judgment time God withholds the fullness of the awesome greatness of the Divine from the soul being judged, yet pierces the darkened mind in some indirect way so that it realizes what has been lost. Hence the primary pain of Hell: a sense of permanent deprivation of the Beatific Vision.

What then about Hell's physical punishment, fire?

Traditional answer: that's the secondary pain of Hell, and no mere metaphorical fire is it of pain over the loss of God. It is real fire, the pains of which in Arendzen's words "exceed in horror all that men can imagine." But does not fire consume what it burns, eventually reducing the object to ashes? Therefore, would not at some time or another the agony come to an end for those condemned to Hell, since they would be burned to ashes? Yesterday's theologian replied: "the bodies of the damned do not disintegrate."

Another difficulty: how can the body burn when the body isn't supposed to be united to the soul until the Last or General Judgment? How can a body that isn't physically present experience pain? How, indeed, can fire affect a soul, which is pure spirit? Answer: Hell's fire "affects even the demons, who are pure spirits, and the damned, who until the General Resurrection, are without their terrestrial bodies." This occurs through "God's omnipotence" in making fire directly act on a pure intelligence.

All this presumably being known, where then is Hell? Hell is a place, but yesterday's theologian is not certain where in the universe it is. Hell was once thought to be in the center of the earth, but that was a while back in time, when knowledge of geography was elementary. Where Hell is is a mystery. As Arendzen remarked, "it has not pleased God to reveal" where Hell is.

All this Hell business is very bleak, and of course the net sum conveys an impression of a religion of terror and despair, and of a God who is anything but all-loving, but instead retributive and heartless. Small consolation that as in Heaven there are degrees of happiness, so in Hell are there degrees of punishment. That might make God fair, but it doesn't make a condemning God particularly kind. God comes across as a heavy, "a legalistic monster," in one commentator's words.

But again that's all old theology. What do modern theologians say?

Many find the whole idea of Hell incongruous with an all-loving, all-forgiving God, and some even suggest that there's no Hell at all. This is Richard McBrien on the subject: "Neither Jesus, nor the church after him, ever stated that persons actually go to Hell or are there now. He—as does the church—restricts himself to the *possibility.''* (Emphasis McBrien's.)

But aren't the Scriptures full of descriptions of Hell as a place of weeping and gnashing of teeth (Matthew 8:12, etc.), where the worm does not die (Mark 9:48), situated there in ''outer darkness'' (Matthew 25:30, etc.)? Says McBrien, that's imagery used by the Scriptures not to describe a particular place, but rather the urgency of Jesus' proclamation of the Kingdom and the seriousness of the individual's decision for or against the Kingdom. McBrien's bottom line: ''To turn our backs on God is to be finally and fully alienated and estranged from God. It is to choose inauthentic existence. It is to reject community with God and with others. It is to opt for isolation and separation.''

For anyone that, of course, can be one hell of a Hell . . . that is, if that's what Hell is all about.

* * *

Purgatory is a problematic Catholic Christian place.

SORT OF . . . There's a lot about a Heaven and a Hell in the New Testament, but nothing specific about a Purgatory. In fact, Catholic exegetes must go to the Old Testament for their strongest scriptural support of such a place—to 2 Maccabees 12:42ff. and the taking up there of a collection as an expiatory offering for soldiers who had been slain in sin.

Thus it is Jewish belief in the efficacy of prayers for the dead that underpins Catholic teaching in favor of a condition of temporary punishment in a spot called Purgatory for those who have died in God's grace but are not entirely free from so-called venial sin. (With mortal sin, the person is a goner, of course.)

New Testament tracts are cited in support of Purgatory—e.g., Matthew 12:32 and 1 Corinthians 3:11-15—but they require exegesis that many have found strained. Such exegesis exists in abundance, however, as from Augustine in the fourth century and Isidore of Seville in the sixth. There is also the decree of Pope Gregory the Great (590-604) explicitly formulating the doctrine of a Purgatory. But it wasn't until the Councils of Lyons (1274), Florence (1439) and Trent (1545-1563), notably the last, that the doctrine was finally nailed down.

Trent defined as follows: ''Whereas the Catholic Church, instructed by the Holy Spirit, has from the Sacred Scripture and the ancient tradition of the Fathers taught in the Councils and very recently in this Ecumenical synod that there is a Purgatory, and that the souls therein detailed are helped by the suffrages of the faithful, but principally by the acceptable Sacrifice of the Altar; the Holy Synod enjoins on the bishops that they diligently endeavor to have the sound doctrine of the Fathers in Councils regarding Purgatory everywhere taught and preached, held and believed by the faithful.''

Not everyone was buying. Like the early Gnostics and the Waldenses and Albinenses of the Middle Ages, the churches of the Reformation, with the exception of a small group of Anglicans, unanimously rejected the idea of a Purgatory, affirming to the contrary that ''the souls of believers are at their death made perfect in holiness and do immediately pass into glory.'' That concept is a concrete application of the Protestant principle of justification by faith, as opposed to Catholic doctrine of justification by works.

The Orthodox Church rejects the notion of a Purgatory, but does believe in an intermediate state after death—a nuance which may reduce to one of semantics rather than theology. The disagreement between East and West is centered in the main over what happens in this middle or intermediate state. Since Saints Thomas Aquinas and Bonaventure, Catholic theory has generally held that the souls of the faithful departed are purified by a material fire. The Orthodox have never accepted that idea, and some Catholic theologians are themselves coming around to that position.

Indeed, Andrew Greeley in *The Bottom Line Catechism* (Thomas More, 1982) holds that the doctrine of Purgatory is a wise and far more consoling teaching, "especially when Purgatory is no longer painted as one of the outer suburbs of Hell with the 'poor' souls shrieking in agony and suffering as they occasionally did in some of the more imaginative catechetical classes of the preconciliar church." (Augustine contended that the sufferings of Purgatory were greater than the sufferings of all the martyrs, and Thomas Aquinas argued that the least pain in Purgatory's fires was greater than the greatest pain on earth.)

Purgatory remains very much a Catholic doctrine, as the Feast of All Souls on November 2 makes abundantly clear. But at the same time Purgatory is really a pious Catholic tradition. It is not an article of faith.

* * *

Like Purgatory, Limbo is pious Catholic imagery.

TRUE . . . In point of fact, Limbo is a Middle Ages idea, a solution to a problem that had stumped theologians from the moment they defined baptism as necessary for salvation on the authority of Christ's admonition to Nicodemus: "Verily, verily, I say unto thee, Except a man be born of water and of the Spirit, he cannot enter unto the kingdom of God" (John 3:5).

This being so of baptism, what then was the fate of those who died as infants before the sacrament could be administered? Were those infants to be excluded from heaven? Augustine said yes, and other early church fathers took their lead from him: unbaptized infants suffered a form of damnation. Indeed, Augustine held that unbaptized infants suffered a kind of positive pain, though what that was he confessed to not knowing, except he thought it would be light and easily bearable.

For many such a fate, however light and bearable the pain, smacked of cruel and unusual punishment. Further, it was inconsistent with the mercy of an all-loving God.

But how did one get around John 3:5?

The answer was provided by the person known as the father of scholasticism, Anselm of Canterbury (1033-1109). Unbaptized infants, he concluded, did not go to heaven, but they weren't damned either; rather they went to a place of peace and natural happiness, where their only, albeit great, loss was deprivation of the beatific vision, the full flowering of grace. This place was just outside heaven or on its border—*in limbo*, in the Latin. Hence the theology, hence the name.

Still the question was not completely settled. Pope Pius V in 1567 had to condemn the teaching of Michael du Bay of Louvain that unbaptized infants, attaining the use of reason after death, would hate and blaspheme God, thus making Limbo a place filled with malcontents set against God's law. Two centuries later, Pope Pius VI had to reject a teaching of the Erastian Synod held at Pistoia in Tuscany which dismissed ''the

Limbo of the infants'' as a ''Pelagian fable.'' That was 1794.

On the other hand, whereas popes have condemned discounters of Limbo, neither pope nor the church itself has ever formally defined Limbo. Vatican II, for instance, spoke at length on God's saving will and human conscience, but it never alluded to a Limbo. Limbo, in sum, is merely a general teaching of theologians. Its status in the hierarchy of ecclesiastical truths, as Joseph Martos comments in *Doors to the Sacred* (Doubleday, 1981), is that of ''a workable solution to a sticky problem.''

Workable, but then how satisfactory? Even with a Limbo the unbaptized infant is still lost, as English theologian Canon George D. Smith pointed out back in 1949 in *The Teachings of the Catholic Church* (Macmillan). ''He is not in some midway state between salvation and damnation,'' Smith commented in then-common gender inclusive style. ''He was made for one end only, a supernatural end; and failure to reach that, whether the fault be his own or another's, is complete failure, is eternal loss, even though unaccompanied by the positive tortures of a soul that has willfully damned itself.''

Nothing's changed since then. Limbo remains a pious Catholic tradition, and not a very satisfactory one at that.

II

Worship

Worship is the reverence due to God. In many respects it is duty; in all respects it is loyalty. The highest homage is that of the mind, for through the mind one knows God and directs the will whereby one loves God and subordinates oneself to God's will. Yet the individual also expresses himself or herself personally and in exterior ways; that is, through prayer and acts of reverence, most notably the liturgy, the official worship of the church. There are, of course, interior as well as exterior forms of worship, and they are attended by aids deriving from the knowledge and experiences of creation. There is, finally, a strong institutional element in worship, for the church as institution originates and fosters various components of worship.

John Deedy

The Sign of the Cross, the gesture of individuals tracing Christ's cross from head to chest and shoulder to shoulder, is a much more elaborate motion now than it was in the early church.

TRUE . . . The Sign of the Cross was common among Christians by the second century, but it seems originally to have involved on the unobtrusive tracing of the cross on the forehead with the thumb or forefinger.

The more elaborate gesture seems an indirect result of the Monophysite heresy of the fifth century, which rejected the two natures of Christ, human and divine, and argued instead for a single composite nature. In essence, Monophysitism was a denial of Christ's human nature. Monophysitism was condemned by the Council of Chalcedon in 451. In symbolic support of the teaching upheld by the Council, Catholics started blessing themselves with two fingers of the right hand—the forefinger and middle finger, or the thumb and middle finger—the action thus typifying the two natures and therefore two wills of Christ.

But if symbolic gesture this was to be, some more perceptible Sign of the Cross was in order than a relatively inconspicuous one to the forehead alone. Hence came the practice of tracing the cross from forehead to breast, shoulder to shoulder. At shoulder level, the hand moved from right shoulder to left, as it still does today in the Eastern church.

Facts, Myths and Maybes

The right to left movement appears to have had no particular significance apart from continuing the right to left movement of the tracing of the Sign of the Cross on one's forehead. The hand just seemed to move more naturally that way.

Later in the East, the third finger was added to the Sign of the Cross as a symbol of the three persons of the Trinity, the gesture now involving thumb, forefinger and middle finger, with ring finger and little finger folded into the palm.

None of this is the way of the Western church today, of course, though it had been well into the twelfth and thirteenth centuries. Sculpture and pictures of the period show the Sign of the Cross being made with three fingers, and though there was no such thing then as cameras or moving pictures, the presumption is that at the shoulders the hand moved from right to left.

Before the close of the Middle Ages, however, Catholics of the West were blessing themselves with the open hand and tracing the bar of the cross not from right to left, but exactly the opposite, left to right. Natural hand movement in the East was apparently not the same in the West. In any instance, the Trinity association was preserved with the invocation joined to the Sign of the Cross, ''In the name of the Father, and of the Son, and of the Holy Spirit.''

Thus the matter stands. The old Monophysite Association is dead, or long forgotten. More current associa-

John Deedy

tions have succeeded its link to the Sign of the Cross. As the old Catechism reminds, the Sign of the Cross is important; it "expresses our belief in the chief mysteries of our faith because: (1) the words we say show that God is one in three divine persons; (2) the cross we make reminds us that Jesus Christ, the Son of God, died for us on the cross."

* * *

The believing, worshiping people of God are gathered into a union of fellowship and sisterhood, a spiritual solidarity known as the Communion of the Saints.

FACT . . . The Communion of the Saints is the unifying liturgical principle that is the bond of the church, the Mystical Body of Christ, the latter so called because its members are joined by supernatural ties with one another and with Christ, thus resembling the members and head of a living human body. That's a bit involved, but it's also elementary. The teaching is found in every elementary catechism.

The Communion of the Saints, then, is a participation in a common faith. It is the interlocking exchange of graces, blessings, merits, satisfactions, good works, prayers, sacramental life, etc., one that exists between the church triumphant (those in Heaven), the church militant (those on earth), and the church suffering (those in that place Catholics call Purgatory). To the extent that there is an emphasis within the union it is on the word communion. The church is a communion ordained by God the Father, in Christ the Son, through the power of the Spirit—the Trinity operative.

This principle is an article of the Apostles Creed: ". . . I believe in the Holy Spirit, the holy Catholic church, *the communion of saints*, the resurrection of the body, and the life everlasting." It is also an affirmation of Vatican Council II (1962-1965). The affirmation is contained in the Dogmatic Constitution on the Church, *Lumen gentium*, although curiously the term "Communion of the Saints" is not used, nor is there an explicit reference to Purgatory. Nonetheless *Lumen gentium* is clear enough. It speaks thus:

"For all who belong to Christ, having his Spirit, form one church and cleave together in him (cf. Ephesians 4:16). Therefore the union of the wayfarers with the brethren who have gone to sleep in the peace of Christ is not in the least interrupted. On the contrary, according to the perennial faith of the church, it is strengthened through the exchanging of spiritual goods" (49). Those in Heaven, because they are more closely united with Christ, "establish the whole church more firmly in holiness, lend nobility to the worship which the church offers on earth to God, and in many ways contribute to its greater upbuilding (cf. 1 Corinthians 12:12-27) . . . [By] their brotherly

interest our weakness is very greatly strengthened''
(49).

As for the church suffering, *Lumen gentium* comments: ''Very much aware of the bonds linking the
whole Mystical Body of Jesus Christ, the pilgrim church
from the very first ages of the Christian religion has
cultivated with great piety the memory of the dead.
Because it is 'a holy and wholesome thought to pray
for the dead that they may be loosed from sins' (2 Maccabees 12:46), she has also offered prayers for them''
(50).

Lumen gentium proceeds to speak of the Apostles and
martyrs, the Virgin Mary and the saints, and notes that
''just as Christian communion among wayfarers brings
us closer to Christ, so our companionship with the
saints joins us to Christ, from whom as from their foun-
tain and head issue every grace and the life of God's
people itself'' (50).

* * *

The Mass is the Catholic Church's central act of worship.

FACT . . . The Mass is indeed the principal act of worship of the Catholic faith. It is a liturgical ceremony of
commemoration and of celebration, the essential feature of which is the transubstantiation or changing of
bread and wine into the body and blood of Christ.

Facts, Myths and Maybes

In the understanding of the Council of Trent (1545-1563), the Mass continues the sacrifice of the cross—in fact, is identical with it, the one difference being that, while the sacrifice of the cross was a bloody sacrifice, that of the Mass is an unbloody sacrifice, the body and blood of Christ becoming present under the appearances of bread and wine. Like the sacrifice of the cross, that of the Mass atones for the sins of the living and the dead, specifically those for whom it is offered.

Trent's understanding carried over several centuries, disturbed only by some minor discussion over whether the Mass was an actual "reenactment" of Calvary or a "re-presentation" of the crucifixion and death of Christ. The reenactment theory was the predominant one.

Vatican Council II (1962-1965) shifted ground. It returned to the Mass an understanding common in the early centuries; that is, of a sacred meal, but also a festive one—albeit not so festive as once upon a time it was at Corinth. Remember how Saint Paul had to warn against abuses at the sacramental meal? Seems some people were getting drunk at the Mass, and some were going hungry because people were not sharing the food of the table with everyone (1 Corinthians 2:17-34).

Well, Vatican II didn't suggest a return to that kind of sacred meal or Mass, but it did reemphasize that the

Mass, in addition to being a memorial of Christ's death and resurrection, was "a sacrament of love, a sign of unity, a bond of charity, a paschal banquet in which Christ is consumed, the mind is filled with grace, and a pledge of future glory is given to us" (*Sancrosanctum concilium,* Constitution on the Sacred Liturgy, 47). It is this emphasis of thanksgiving and shared eucharistic meal that the new liturgy seeks to bring to the Mass.

Under the new liturgy, the Mass consists of two divisions: the Liturgy of the Word and the Eucharistic Liturgy. The former features readings that are in essence the proclamation of the Word of God; the latter, the consecration and sharing of the eucharistic meal. (Formerly, the divisions were known as the Mass of the Catechumens and the Mass of the Faithful.) Additionally, there are ancillary introductory and concluding rites, such as the entrance antiphon, penetential rite, doxology of glory to God, prayers and blessing of dismissal. And, of course, the primary language of the Mass is now the local vernacular.

* * *

The Our Father is the basic prayer of Roman Catholicism—in fact, of all Christianity.

FACT . . . The Our Father, or Lord's Prayer, is the prayer that Christ himself taught, and is found in the long Sermon on the Mount that began with the Beatitudes and ranged over a score of topics, which we are told left the crowds "spellbound." What most people do not know is that there are two forms to the prayer.

There's the familiar one of Matthew's gospel (6:9-13): "Our Father who are in Heaven, hallowed be thy name. Thy kingdom come, thy will be done, on earth as it is in Heaven. Give us this day our daily bread, and forgive us our trespasses, as we forgive those who trespass against us. And lead us not into temptation, but deliver us from evil."

There's also Luke's version (11:2-4): "Father, hallowed be thy name. Thy kingdom come. Give us each day our daily bread; and forgive us our sins, for we ourselves forgive every one who is indebted to us; and lead us not into temptation" (Revised Standard Version, Catholic Edition, 1965).

At some point the doxology came to be added to the prayer, "For thine is the kingdom, and the power, and the glory, forever and forever, Amen." This is commonly thought by Catholics to be a Protestant addition to the prayer, and not surprisingly since its first major appearance was in the King James Version of the Bible of the early seventeenth century. The fact is, however, that the doxology is much older, and was likely added by a pious monk back before the days of the printing press, when bibles were copied by hand. The doxology had the ring of Scripture, and thus the addition came to be perpetuated. King James' scholars, unaware that the doxology was not scriptural, included it in their version as the closing words of the prayer.

The doxology, quite beautiful, is now included in Catholic eucharistic liturgies, though separated from the Our Father. Protestants continue to use the doxology as part of the Our Father itself, although some bibles omit the phrase or footnote it to indicate that the phrase was added by ancient authorities.

* * *

The Hail Mary dates back almost as far as the Our Father.

MYTH . . . To be sure, the seeds of devotion to Mary were sprouting by the second century, but not the prayer, the Hail Mary.

Indeed, it was not until around 1050, the eleventh century, that the devout began shaping the scriptural salutations of the Annunciation story—"Hail Mary, full of grace, the Lord is with thee. Blessed are thou amongst women, and blessed is the fruit of thy womb" (Luke 1:26-28, 1:42)—into a prayer. Further, it was not until the sixteenth century that the petition was formally added, "Holy Mary, Mother of God, pray for us sinners, now and at the hour of our death. Amen."

A note of irony: the oldest known formula of the Hail Mary corresponding to ours (except for the omission of a single word, *nostrae*) is at the head of a work issued in 1495 in the possession of the British Museum. The work was by Girolamo Savanarola, the Dominican reformer and hairshirt of Alexander VI, who was hanged in 1498, his body burned, and the ashes cast into the Arno at Florence.

* * *

The rosary originated as a serial recitation of Our Fathers, not Hail Marys.

FACT . . . and the devotion was known as the Paternosters, after the first two words of the Latin Our Father, *Pater noster*. In fact, the rosary gained currency only with the explosion of Marian devotion in the Middle Ages. The Hail Mary was substituted for the Our Father, and the new devotion drew its name from the popular medieval appellation for Mary, Mystical Rose.

But back to the beginning . . .

From time immemorial the devout of all religions used a system to keep count of prayers. The fourth-century hermit Paul kept count with pebbles, casting one away as each prayer was finished until at last there were none. Muslims and Buddhists strung beads on a string and moved their fingers from one to the next until finished, and so in time did Catholic Christians—first for the Paternosters; afterwards for the Hail Marys.

Keeping count was important, as particular circumstances dictated the saying of precise numbers of prayers. For instance, the "Ancient Customs of Cluny"

(1096) required priests to offer mass and non-priests to say fifty psalms or fifty Our Fathers on the death of a colleague. Knights Templar unable to attend choir were required to say fifty-seven Our Fathers.

As for the rosary, it began as a 150-prayer devotion and gained popularity through the preaching of Saint Dominic (1170-1221) to counter the Albigensian heresy. It was not until two centuries after Dominic's death, however, that the rosary took the form known today. It was subdivided for meditative purposes into fifty-prayer devotions of five decades, each grouped around three sets of mysteries, the joyful, sorrowful and glorious.

The popularity of the rosary has waned in recent years, but it is still common for Catholics to exit this world with the rosary entwined between their fingers.

*   *   *

The church's institutional structure was bequeathed to it by its founder, Jesus.

MYTH . . . The institutional church developed totally independent of Jesus. Further, the structure of the modern church, from the diocesan level through to the Vatican itself, would be unrecognizable to the fathers of the earliest church. So would terms like "bishop" and "diocese." The four Evangelists did not use them. The earliest church spoke instead of local churches, and of leaders as shepherds or guardians. Further, local churches had different governing structures, and the leaders of these churches were not known as bishops at least until the first epistle of Peter. Even then there is some question about the latter. Some translators render a reference in 1 Peter 2:25 as "bishop," but others as "guardian." Given the context (Peter is speaking of sheep who had strayed), the rendering as "bishop" appears to be license. Look it up for yourself.

That's not all. Far more unrecognizable to the church fathers, and indeed to Jesus himself, would be the church's central government, and most especially the independent political entity known as the State of Vatican City.

The State of Vatican City is the remnant of the militarily and diplomatically powerful Papal States that existed from 754 to 1870, and extended throughout much of what is known now as central Italy. It has existed in its present form only since the Lateran Concordat of 1929 with Fascist Italy. As a state, the Vatican is miniscule—only 108.7 acres, hardly the size of a small mid-western American farm. To many it is more a museum than a state, but that is not how governments around the world view it. Some one hundred and twenty-five governments maintain diplomatic relations with the Vatican, including most of those recently loosened from communist rule.

Some persons wonder why a territory that is really

the headquarters of a church should want to be sovereign and independent.

The church's position is that territorial independence protects the pope's religious independence and increases his freedom to carry out a worldwide mission. The church also feels that territorial independence enables the pope to communicate with the whole world on political and economic themes, in addition to those of religion and theology.

The reverse of the coin—and particularly crucial in the recent past when some governments were hostile to religion and others anxious to preserve principles of separation of church and state—is that territorial independence provides countries with the option of negotiating with a government rather than a church. One such country, of course, is the United States, which restored diplomatic relations with the Vatican in 1984.

* * *

The term Roman Catholic is an oxymoron, an intrinsic contradiction.

FACT . . . In the sense that the word "Catholic" in its basic meaning denotes universality and that "Roman" as a modifying adjective indicates a particularity, the term is indeed an oxymoron. Yet the term is applied as one of identity for Catholics generally. As such, the term is a misnomer—in fact, in the opinion of some, a near pejorative.

The term came into existence in the eleventh century as a distinction between Catholics of the East and those of the West, and gained wider currency in the sixteenth century as the term identifying those who remained loyal to Rome instead of joining the Protestant Reformation. For some, notably English recusants—those who refused to renounce allegiance to Rome—the term was a badge of honor. For others—those in much of the rest of the reforming world—the term came to be widely viewed as a disparagement delimiting their Catholicity, narrowing it to the context of loyalty to the pope or bishop of Rome. For many of today's Catholics (although not all, and certainly not conservative Catholics), it is still seen as an aspersion.

Yet, the term "Roman Catholic" has valid usages—as, for instance, in identifying those belonging to the Church's Roman or Latin Rite. The Roman Rite is the prevalent rite of the Western Church, but still only one among many rites in the church as a whole. There are the Eastern Rites (the Byzantine, Alexandrian, Antiochene, Armenian and Chaldean), as well as sub-rites within the Western Church (Ambrosian, Mozarabic, Lyonnais, Braga and several monastic rites associated with religious orders). Thus there are all kinds of Catholics besides "Roman Catholics."

Whatever their rite, the most accurate way for

117

John Deedy

Catholic believers to describe themselves is simply as "Catholics." It's a more ecumenical term. It's also historically precise, and has been since the Council of Nicaea, 325.

* * *

Mary named her son Jesus Christ, according to the instruction of the angel Gabriel.

HALF-FACT . . . What the angel Gabriel said to Mary was, "Thou shalt conceive in thy womb, and bring forth a son, and shall call his name Jesus" (Luke 1:31). Thus was the son known. The angel did not mention the word Christ.

Christ then was not a proper name, but rather a title, meaning "the anointed one." In the scriptures, accordingly, the word Christ is commonly (though not invariably) preceded by the article *the;* e.g., Peter responding to the question, "But whom say ye that I am?": ". . . Thou art the Christ, the Son of the Living God" (Matthew 16:15-16). It was only after the Resurrection that the title Christ began to be used as a proper name, and that the expression Jesus Christ or Christ Jesus became the one designation.

The word Jesus, incidentally, is the Latin form of a proper name that transliterates through the Greek to the Hebrew word *Jeshua* or *Joshua,* meaning "Jehovah is salvation." That in turn telescopes to savior.

Facts, Myths and Maybes

Jesus was an only child, meaning he had no brothers and sisters.

TRUE . . . according to official Catholic teaching, that is. But not everyone is so sure on the point. There's a school of thought, primarily Protestant but including individual Catholic scholars like Father John P. Meier of the Catholic University of America, which holds that Jesus had several siblings—as many as four brothers and at least two sisters.

The very possibility of such a circumstance jars traditionalist sensibilities. However, the New Testament is replete with references to "brethren" or brothers of the Lord (Matthew 12:46, 13:55; Mark 3:31-32; Luke 8:19-20; John 2:12, etc.), and to a "sister" or "sisters" of Jesus (Mark 6:3; 1 Corinthians 9:5). The sister or sisters are given no name, but the "brethren" or brothers are identified as James, Joseph or Joses, Simon and Jude. Citing but one example, this is Saint Paul on the subject of possible siblings of Jesus. In Galatians 1:19: "But other of the apostles saw I none, save James the Lord's brother."

For most Protestants there is no theological difficulty in Jesus having a brother or sister, or several of each. In fact, it is general Protestant belief that the family of Mary and Joseph was a large one. In official Catholicism, on the other hand, the thought is anathema, for if Mary had multiple births, gone is teaching about

119

John Deedy

Mary's perpetual virginity, and into question comes everything connected with the virgin birth. Marian theology, in a word, would have to be rewritten from chapter one.

There is no disputing that the references to "brother" and "sister" appear in the original Greek of the New Testament. So what's the Catholic explanation for the usage? It is that the terms were used to indicate relatives who were cousins of Jesus. In literal context, "brethren" does indeed mean "brothers." But, say Catholic spokespersons, the word is merely a carry-over from the Aramaic of the first Christians. In that language "brothers" designated a closely defined group, such as cousins or other distant relatives. Since Aramaic, like Hebrew, had no word for "cousin," it would be logical then to adopt the word brother or sister in its stead. A modern-day parallel would be the use of the words "brothers" and "sisters" by Afro-Americans as a generic term designating members of their population group.

Of course it is possible that, as an older man, Joseph was married before his spouseship with Mary, and that the brothers and sisters alluded to in the New Testament were children from such a union and therefore stepbrothers and stepsisters of Jesus. Catholic exegesis rejects this notion as well, however, contending that the heritage of two of the "brethren" (James and Joseph or Joses) can be specifically traced to other parents, and concluding that if those two were not the brothers or stepbrothers of Jesus, neither were any of the others—a conclusion some find sweeping in the leap from two to all.

Apart from the direct scriptural references to brothers and sisters, there's the difficulty of Matthew 1:25 ("And [he] knew her not till she had brought forth her firstborn son") and Luke 2:7 ("And she brought forth her firstborn son"). For many these texts imply that Mary had borne a daughter or daughters before having Jesus, and that likely she had more children after Jesus. The Catholic response is (1) that the term "firstborn son" does not necessarily connote that other children were born earlier or later, and (2) that an only child is no less a "firstborn" than a senior sibling would be.

But perhaps the strongest refutation of the brothers and sisters theory isn't in scriptural exegesis, but rather is sociological in nature.

In a word, where in the world were all these brothers and sisters when Jesus was crucified and they were presumably needed the most for comfort and support? Wouldn't it have been logical, if they existed, for them to be there at the foot of the cross with Mary, their mother? And if brothers and sisters there were, why would it have been necessary for Jesus on his cross to commend the care of his mother to John (John 19:26-27: "Woman, behold thy son! Then saith he to the disciple, Behold thy mother!'')? True, John was Jesus' favorite disciple, but he was still a family outsider in the context of duty to one's parent.

It's possible, perhaps, that all of the siblings died between their mention in the stories of Jesus' public life and his death on the cross, but that's a pack of dying in a couple of years' time with no mention being made. Then again, maybe the brothers and sisters were all alienated from Jesus? But that doesn't square, does it, with Jesus' temperament and the picture of domestic tranquillity that we're told prevailed in the Holy Family?

The bottom line: Go with traditionalist opinion.

* * *

Clerical celibacy is a discipline, not a doctrine of the church, and one that dates only from the Middle Ages.

TRUE . . . Celibacy as a condition of ordination is indeed a latter-day discipline, although the concept of a celibate clergy did build on conclusions of very early local church councils, beginning with Elvira in Spain between 295 and 302, then including councils at Rome, Turin, Toledo and Carthage, among others. Individual popes added the authority of the papacy in favor of celibacy, a few by measures that can only be viewed now as benighted. For instance, Pope Benedict VIII (1012-1024) discouraged clerical marriages by declaring the children of such unions serfs of the church, with no rights of property or inheritance, while Pope Innocent III (1198-1216) did so by effectively labeling clerical wives concubines and adultresses. "Priests are supposed to be God's temples, vessels of the Lord and sanctuaries of the Holy Spirit [and] it offends their dignity to lie in the conjugal bed and live in impunity," said Innocent at the Synod of Clermont. There was much worse. A London synod in 1108 declared the wives of priests to be property of the bishop, and a 1231 synod at Rouen ordered the hair of clerical wives cut off at public church ceremonies, much as after World War II the French would cut off the hair of women who had collaborated with the Nazis. The Rouen action, extra tough as it was, was also superfluous, because by then the tide had been turned against a married clergy.

The issue had been long up for grabs, because Jesus of course said nothing on the subject of celibacy. To be sure St. Paul had. He celebrated celibacy and virginity as a higher calling, urging the unmarried and widows to "abide even as I" (1 Corinthians 7:8-9), and arguing that those in service of the Lord could not serve two masters ("Brethren, the time is short: it remaineth, that both they that have wives be as though they had none, and they that weep, as though they wept not" etc. . . . 1 Cor. 7:29-34). In so writing St. Paul provided clerical celibacy with its scriptural basis.

John Deedy

Two other factors entered into the picture to support opposition to a married clergy. One was simony—more specifically, the practice by some priests of willing or transmitting benefices or ecclesiastical assets to their children; such incidents had built into a problem of considerable proportions. The second factor was the persistent attitude at the church's leadership levels that sexual intercourse, even in a conjugal situation, was unholy and defiling. The logical step was to insure that those who celebrated the liturgy and handled the consecrated body of Christ were walled off from such unholiness and defilement, and celibacy was the means for doing so. Thus even before clerical marriages were outlawed entirely, married clergy were directed to live with their spouses as brother and sister.

As might be noted apropos the latter, similar sexual attitudes did not exist in the Eastern church, and still don't. Clerical marriages are recognized in Eastern uniate rites if contracted before ordination to the diaconate. At one time, Rome was hostile toward this tradition—the head of an eleventh-century papal delegation to a critical ecumenical conference in Constantinople going so far on one occasion to rail against "young husbands, just now exhausted with carnal lust, serving at the altar." Rome continues to hold the line against a married clergy in the Roman or Latin Rite, but it has come to accept the reality that exists a few degrees of longitude eastwards. Vatican II, for instance, praised the "outstanding merit" of married priests who serve in the Eastern church, and pledged that "it in no way intends to change that different discipline which lawfully prevails" there (*Presbyterorum Ordinis*, Decree on the Ministry and Life of Priests, 16).

Leo IX (1049-1054) and Gregory VII (1073-1085) were the pontiffs who were decisive in fixing church policy on celibacy—probably especially Gregory, the Hildebrand pope, for it was he who banned all clerics involved in a sexual union with women from the very exercise of ministry. As *praepositus* (provisor) of St. Paul Outside the Walls before his election to the papacy, Hildebrand had ended the practice of monks being attended in the refectory by women, so his feelings about women in clerical milieus could be presumed at the time of his election as pope. Predictably, he took the issue full course.

After Gregory, the weight of ecumenical councils began to mass on the side of celibacy. Lateran Councils I and II (1123 and 1139, respectively) not only forbade clerical marriages, but declared those marriages contracted after ordination null *pleno jure*; it was deemed, in effect, that a priest was incapable of marriage. Synodal gatherings added further condemnations and prohibitions against clerical marriages, then Trent (1545-1563) anathematized "anyone [who] says that it is not better and more godly to live in virginity or in the unmarried state than to marry."

John Deedy

With Trent the matter seemed settled. Railings and exhortations were no longer necessary. It was enough now to celebrate celibacy in terms of what it had come to mean in the Western church: the life of perfect chastity undertaken in total dedication to the service of God and people. Vatican II entered into that celebration. No sooner had the council ended, however, than did challenges to the discipline once again become commonplace. Thousands of priests rejected celibacy by leaving the priesthood for marriage. Compounding Rome's problem was the divided attitude among many of those who stayed, for suddenly there was questioning in the ranks whether celibacy should be a mandatory or an optional discipline.

The response of the papacy has been interesting. Paul VI deplored those probing the celibacy discipline, telling them ''there were better things to do'' with their time. Yet he was lenient toward those who felt they could not live the discipline, approving the laicizations of some 32,000 priests worldwide. John Paul II, by contrast, has been much sterner. ''Celibacy is not simply a juridical addition to the sacrament of orders,'' he said during a 1984 visit to Switzerland. ''It is a commitment of the person, taken in full maturity, to Christ and the church.'' He insists this commitment be honored. Consistent with that attitude, he toughened the laicization process, for a time shutting it down completely. There has been an easing of policy of late, but no return to the leniency of Paul VI. In 1990, for instance, there were reports of a so-called "laicization-jam" amounting to as many as 10,000 cases.

Summing up, clerical celibacy is a discipline of the church, not a dogma; it is a requisite of the Western church, not of the Eastern church; it can be easily waived, and frequently has been, as in 1981 to accommodate a number of married Anglican priests who converted to Roman Catholicism rather than serve alongside women clergy in Episcopalianism. As for the current pope, he is emphatic on the subject. Whatever the pressures of ministry or force of argument, clerical celibacy can be expected to stay as long as John Paul II reigns.

By way of footnote, it might be noted that one of the options offered in 1992 by Rome to Czechoslovak married men, who were secretly ordained during the communist ascendancy and had second careers as priests, was service in the Greek Catholic or another uniate church. The Eastern discipline thus provided an answer to a difficult Western dilemma. Might it be the answer for others down the line, such as that of vocations?

* * *

If in our age the church's mandatory celibacy requirement for priests inhibits the development of new vocations, as some allege, the consequences won't be all negative, for fewer priests

127

John Deedy

will only energize further traditional Catholic concepts of the "priesthood of the laity."

PERHAPS . . . although it is difficult to conceive of that energizing as a magic formula or divine blessing solving all problems.

The priesthood of the laity, as remarked by Thomas Aquinas and confirmed by Vatican II's Dogmatic Constitution on the Church, *Lumen gentium,* is a very real concept, but it is still a limited one. It is a priesthood that stems from a sharing in the sacraments of baptism and confirmation, but it has nothing to do whatsoever with holy orders. The priesthood of the laity and the ministerial or hierarchical priesthood are "common" or "interrelated," and "each of them in its own special way is a participation in the one priesthood of Christ"—*Lumen gentium,* 10. At the same time, as *Lumen gentium* tells us, "they differ from one another in essence and not only in degree." The ministerial or hierarchical priesthood by divine commission serves the universal priesthood; the priesthood of the laity is radically more defined. In it are none of the powers of holy orders for offering Mass and celebrating the Eucharist, or for providing such pastoral care as absolving from sin, confirming, anointing the sick, etc. It is a secondary or auxiliary priesthood at most.

Yet in recent years the priesthood of the laity has been utilized in real and imaginative ways, both under the positive impetus of Vatican II and the pragmatic necessities of the clergy shortage. Laity are performing all sorts of ministerial tasks once associated exclusively with priests, such as the distribution of communion at Mass and to shut-ins. More pentinently, laity are also functioning as religious counselors, retreat leaders and directors of religious instruction. They hold high official positions in chancery offices and parish rectories, and they lead the worshiping community in a variety of nonsacramental ceremonies, such as Bible vigils and the extraordinary rite of communion. But, and again it's a very big *but*, they cannot perform those duties without which any Catholic community can hope indefinitely to remain strong and vibrant; they cannot offer Mass and celebrate the Eucharist.

The last detail is especially crucial given the clergy shortage, and the diminishing number of priests available just to meet the traditional Sunday mass obligations of the faithful. A 1988 survey by the U.S. bishops showed that seventy U.S. dioceses have been forced to place parishes or missions under the administration of a deacon, lay person, religious sister or brother, and that parishes or missions in thirty-one of these dioceses were experiencing the phenomenon of priestless Sundays. The situation prompted the bishops to propose to Rome a series of guidelines for the conducting of Sunday worship services in the absence of a priest. The options included morning or evening prayer of the liturgy of the hours, or a liturgy of the word—services which could stand alone or be followed by administration of a pre-consecrated eucharistic host. Rome approved, stating a number of conditions, but nonetheless allowing "Sunday celebrations [to] be led by deacons or by suitably prepared lay people."

All this is very helpful, but is does not answer the long-range problem—the shortage of priests. The problem is serious, and across the United States the picture is not expected to brighten in the foreseeable future. The number of active priests lessens year to year, and clerical deaths and retirements are not being balanced by increases in vocations. The Diocese of Worcester, Massachusetts, to cite but one instance, said recently that over the next four years it will have four more retirements than it has seminarians to replace them, a deficit which does not provide for any deaths, early retirements or seminary drop-outs. It is impossible to put a glow on situations like that, even with broadest understandings and most positive usages of the "priesthood of the laity."

Is the future of American Catholicism, therefore, in jeopardy?

One can only respond by thinking back to the situation that existed in America before the age of immigration brought a large supply of European priests to the U.S. on those tidal waves of peoples, notably from Ireland, Germany and Italy. Before that development, the U.S. was liturgically starved for lack of priests, and in that context the country's first bishop, John Carroll, wrote to Rome about the observance of the laity. In general, he said, American Catholics "are rather faithful to the practices of their religion, and in frequenting the sacraments. All fervor, however, is lacking . . . since many congregations attend mass and hear a sermon [only] once a month or every two weeks. To this extent we are overwhelmed by the scarcity of priests."

Will the past become the future in American Catholicism? Will the consequences of priestless Sundays sap the "fervor" of American Catholics tomorrow as in Carroll's time? To be sure, revitalized concepts of the priesthood of the laity will help allay the threat, but for how long? That is the real question, and no one has the answer.

*   *   *

The permanent diaconate is an emergency measure in response to the vocations crisis, and the office is to be suppressed once priestly vocations are again plentiful.

MYTH . . . The decision to restore the permanent diaconate stems from a recommendation of Vatican Council II (1962-1965), when vocations were generally quite ample. Granted there was a touch of pragmatism to the council's recommendation, and indeed in many dioceses the permanent diaconate has become an answer of sorts to the priest shortage. But the restoration of the permanent diaconate was not initiated as an emergency measure. Council fathers reflected on the permanent diaconate in the Dogmatic Constitution on the Church, *Lumen gentium,* and urged its restoration as an independent clerical order—not only to supply ministers for carrying on the work of the church, but more specifically to return the hierarchical structure of the church of the Roman Rite to its original form, which included a permanent diaconate until the sixth century. The council's action obviously envisioned the permanent diaconate as an enduring institution.

Following up on the council, Pope Paul VI (1963-1978) in 1967 promulgated *Sacrum diaconatus ordinem,* the decree formally restoring the office of permanent deacon for individuals wishing to serve in the ordained ministry without going on to the priesthood itself. The decree provided for the ordination of married men as permanent deacons, of course. But once ordained their status is so different that church law forbids a deacon's remarrying, even on the death of a spouse. In other words, the permanent deaconate is not to be viewed as a wedge toward a non-celibate priesthood.

The reconstitution of the permanent diaconate has been a sensational success, and no where more so than in the U.S., where between 1970 and 1991 the number of permanent deacons has grown from zero to 10,120, and continues to increase by 450 to 500 a year. Within a few years, in fact, there will be one permanent deacon in the U.S. for every three diocesan priests.

That's very high visibility, and it translates to broad ministry. As ordained clerics, permanent deacons can bless marriages, officiate at baptisms, wakes and funerals, bring Viaticum to the dying, preach, act as custodians and dispensers of the Eucharist, conduct liturgies of the Word and preside at worship; they can counsel and instruct, and perform a host of other ministerial, charitable and pastoral duties.

On the other hand—and the distinction is crucial—permanent deacons cannot celebrate Mass, anoint the sick, or hear confessions and absolve from sins (that is, reconcile a person sacramentally). Permanent deacons, in sum, can do so much and no more.

Yet there is so much they can do in terms of ministry, that acceptance of the order on all levels of church would seem virtually automatic. Mostly it is. The Archdiocese of Chicago had 682 permanent deacons as of 1992. New York had 289; Hartford, 270; Newark, 224; Galveston-Houston, 200. In all, twenty-eight U.S. dioceses had 100 or more permanent deacons.

But there's another side to the coin. As of 1992, twenty-five of the 188 archdioceses and dioceses of the U.S. had no permanent-diaconate program, and in another dozen or so more the programs were on hold for a variety of reasons. As one hold-back bishop,

John Deedy

Norbert F. Gaughan of the Diocese of Gary, Indiana, put it in the March, 1992, *U.S. Catholic:* "I just don't know that deacons substitute for priests or that they add that much more to the mix."

Some laity object to the permanent diaconate as "the creation of a class of mini-priests" imposing another layer of clericalism on the church; some find the gender exclusions offensive, since under the present discipline only men may be ordained. Serious points. Still, the order seems here to stay.

* * *

Women once served as deacons in Catholic ministry.

TRUE . . . A number of women had the title of deacon in early Christianity. St. Paul in his letter to the Romans commends Phoebe, "a deaconess of the church of Cenchrae" (16:1), and it is probable that the widows spoken of in 1 Timothy 5:3-10 were also deaconesses. The office existed. Further, the Apostolic Constitutions document that there was a ritual for the ordination of women as deacons that included a laying on of hands, a key element in the ordination rite of men, and modeled in fact on the ritual for the ordination of male deacons. The Apostolic Constitutions detail the prayer of the female ritual thus:

"Concerning a deaconess, I Bartholomew enjoin, O Bishop, thou shalt lay thy hands upon her with all the

Facts, Myths and Maybes

Presbytery and the Deacons and the Deaconesses and thus shalt say: 'Eternal God, the Father of our Lord Jesus Christ, the Creator of man and woman, that didst fill with the Spirit Mary and Deborah, and Anna and Huldah, that didst not disdain that thine only begotten Son should be born of a woman; Thou that in the tabernacle of witness and in the temple didst appoint women guardians of the holy gates: Do Thou now look on this thy handmaid, who is appointed unto the office of a Deaconess and grant unto her the holy Spirit, and cleanse her from all pollution of the flesh and of the spirit, that she may worthily accomplish the work committed unto her, to thy glory and the praise of thy Christ.'''

It is not exactly clear what the work committed to deaconesses was, although it is certain that they had a prominent role in the baptismal rite of women, due to the early prevalence of baptism by immersion. Because the whole body was anointed and the candidate for baptism then led naked into the waters, propriety dictated a special role for them in the baptism of adult females. Whether deaconesses actually baptized is uncertain, but there is no question but that they were widely involved ministerially in the early church, notably in the East where they were known to preside over assemblies of women and perform liturgical functions eventually outlawed.

Progress for women in the church's ministerial areas

John Deedy

continued into the fourth century before being killed by the Council of Nicaea of 325. Nicaea ruled that female deacons were not to be ranked as clergy, but rather as laity engaged in the performance of special missions of service. Though deaconesses continued to be found in the Western church in the fifth century, and in the Eastern church into the sixth century, their days were numbered. Nicaea was the defining moment. It established what was to be a sixteenth-century tradition of exclusion of women from ministerial roles.

Some barriers have been broken down of late, and women are acting in roles that would have boggled eyes just a generation or two ago. They are lectors and commentators at Mass, eucharistic ministers, spiritual advisers, retreat directors, parish administrators, chancery officials, and a host of things more. However, though they act in roles of the ordained, women are not themselves ordained, and in the present church discipline cannot be, most certainly not as priests.

The Vatican's 1977 declaration "On the Question of the Admission of Women to the Ministerial Priesthood" reiterated official position on the latter point, ruling that in the matter of priesthood a "natural resemblance" between Christ and his minister must exist in keeping with the "sacramental sign" of Holy Orders. In a word, a genital qualification existed for the person who "truly acts in the place of Christ." For ordination to the priesthood one had to be male. The

Facts, Myths and Maybes

Vatican declaration did leave open "for the future" the question of women being ordained as deacons, but given the difficulty it has displayed in trying to come to grips with the issue of female acolytes—altar girls—one does not look for an early dawning of that future. In 1980, Pope John Paul II issued an instruction that "women are not allowed the function of a mass-server." That is still official policy, however much it is disregarded at the grassroots.

* * *

The exclusion of women from the formal liturgical life of the church once extended even to song and chant, women being banned as choir members, no matter how beautiful their voices.

TRUE . . . For centuries women were forbidden to sing in church choirs, the grounds being that sacred music was music in the service of the liturgy and liturgy, in turn, was the sacred preserve of men. The place of women was in the congregation, where they were to sit silently with head covered. That comment may seem tendentious, but such is historical fact. As for choirs, if there was need for high soprano and alto voices, it was met by men singing falsetto or, as was the case during certain periods, by *castrati*—young boys sexually mutilated in order that their adolescent soprano and alto voices be preserved. The use of *castrati* was common from the sixteenth to the eighteenth century, especially in Italy, where among other places they were featured in the Sistine Chapel during the reign of Pope Clement VIII (1592-1605).

Society and the church outgrew that aesthetic barbarism, and women in time found their way into church choirs, usually as members of mixed choirs. Still they were exceptions to a regulation rather than persons deserving in their own right as human beings. The ancient mindset persisted that the presence of women in church choirs was liturgically intrusive; choir singers performed a liturgical office, and liturgical offices were reserved for men. In a word, women were included by tolerance.

This mindset carried into this century, and once again women found themselves abruptly excluded from church choirs. Their banning flowed from Pope Pius X's restatement of church policy in *Motu Proprio*, his "Instruction on Sacred Music" of 1903, that women were not to be allowed any liturgical function. As we know from Aunt Kate's protest at the Morkan sisters' Christmastime party in James Joyce's story "The Dead," Catholics were outraged by the pope's action—some, at least. The action did not spoil Pius X's chances of sainthood, however. He was canonized in 1954.

Pius X's exclusion of women from choirs was echoed in the *Repertorium Rituum* of 1912 of Philipp Hartmann, it being stated there that ''Only men of known piety and probity should be permitted to be members of the church choir, men who show themselves worthy of the sacred service.'' If the choir master wished to use high soprano and alto voices, he was told ''boys must be enlisted.''

Pope Pius XII put a dent in this history of discrimination with his 1958 ''Instruction on Sacred Music.'' But though women could now be heard in song in church, it had to be ''outside the presbyterium or the altar rail.'' Actually Pius XII was in effect only acknowledging realities, for women organists, soloists and choir members were already common across Christendom. Certainly they were numerous in the United States.

Looking back, the old policies seem quirky and quaint. From the standpoint of human justice, they are hard to believe, the more so now that church choirs are integrated everywhere, and women not only sing within the presbyterium, but dance and pluck guitars as well. Could the past really have happened? It did, but today's different.

Kate Morkan would be pleased. Too bad that after being chastised for her comments by a niece, she apologized for questioning the pope, and confessed to being ''a stupid old woman.'' Kate Morkan was a herald of the future.

* * *

John Deedy

But did not a woman once serve as pope?

MYTH . . . It is curious to be discussing the possibility of a pope having been a woman, when a woman cannot even be ordained a priest, Holy Orders—and by extension the papacy itself—being the church's one sacrament with a gender exclusion. A male can theoretically receive all seven of the church's sacraments, a widower for instance being eligible for Holy Orders. A woman, as an earlier entry makes clear, is eligible for six of the church's sacraments, but not the seventh, Holy Orders. So what is all this talk about a female pope? Well, it is just that, talk. Except from the mid-thirteenth to the seventeenth century, the tradition of a woman pope was generally believed.

That woman was known as Pope Joan, although not invariably; some records have her as Agnes, Jutta, Gilberta, or just nameless.

Her story first appears in the *Universal Chronicle of Metz* of the Dominican monk Jean de Mailly. According to it Joan was a curia notary who in disguise as a man worked her way into the cardinalate, then the papacy. She is alleged to have succeeded Victor III on his death in 1087, and to have been exposed as a woman when she went into labor while mounting a horse. After giving birth, she is said to have been tied to the horse's tail, dragged about the city of Rome, then stoned to death.

Facts, Myths and Maybes

Another equally vivid account has Pope Joan succeeding Leo IV and occupying the papacy from 855-858. According to this tale, Joan was enamored of the monk Folda, and to be near him assumed the monastic habit. Being shrewd and popular, she advanced in religious life, and to the papacy itself under the name John Anglicus. Her deception was discovered when she gave birth to a child—not secretly, but as fate would have it during a solemn pontifical procession en route from St. Peter's to the Lateran. The setting was a narrow street between the Colosseum and San Clemente. Joan died in childbirth and was buried on the spot. To avoid bad "vibes," popes were said to avoid the street thereafter.

On its face, the story is preposterous, but it enjoyed widespread currency for centuries. Joan figured among the papal busts arranged in the Siena cathedral around 1400, and John Hus invoked the story at the Council of Constance in 1415 without being challenged. A century later Mario Equicola of Alvito was writing that God used Joan's ascendancy to press the point of the equality of women.

Paradoxically, it was not a Catholic researcher who exploded the myth, but a sixteenth-century French Protestant named David Blondel with treatises published in Amsterdam in 1647 and 1657.

What gave rise to the Pope Joan myth in the first place is impossible to say. Oxford scholar J.N.D. Kelly argues in an appendix to his *Oxford Dictionary of Popes* (Oxford, 1986) that the myth was likely rooted in an old Roman folk tale blown out of proportion by several strained suspicions—e.g., the avoidance of a certain street by papal processions (probably only because the street was narrow); the discovery of an enigmatic statue of a woman breast feeding, with a puzzling inscription nearby; and the once common belief from the late thirteenth century that a newly elected pope had to undergo a physical examination to prove he was male. He didn't.

Kelly theorizes further that the myth could have been fed by the recollection that in the tenth century "the papacy had been dominated by unscrupulous women like Theodora the Elder, Marozia, and the younger Theodora."

In any instance, the Pope Joan story is rubbish—interesting rubbish, but rubbish nonetheless.

* * *

It is a "mortal" sin to miss Mass on Sunday.

NOT NOW . . . For one thing, theologians generally don't speak of "mortal" sin anymore; they speak of grave sin or serious sin. But back when they did speak of mortal sin, and when dying in mortal sin meant automatic consignment of one's soul to Hell, the missing of Mass on Sunday, and the holydays as well, was held to be a mortal transgression. The 1938 catechism drawn up under Peter Cardinal Gasparri of the Roman Curia and used throughout the American church made that point abundantly clear. Question and answer number 94 read as follows:

Is it mortal sin to neglect to hear Mass on Sundays and holydays of obligation?

Today the church does not speak in such apocalyptic terms, and it is just as well, for though the Third Commandment of the Lord indeed says, "Remember to keep holy the Sabbath day," it is anything but sure that that commandment obliges the actual hearing of Mass on Sunday—at least unfailingly so.

To be sure, Catholic Christians from earliest times kept Sundays holy as a mark of respect for the Risen Christ, who was believed to have resurrected on the first day of the week. But the first council to address the subject of mandatory Sunday Mass—that of Elvira in 300—seemed only to ask substantial observance of the obligation. It decreed: "If anyone in the city neglects to come to church for three Sundays, let him be excommunicated for a short time so that he may be corrected."

For a thousand years, there was in fact no absolute requirement of Sunday Mass attendance, and when a Lateran Council imposed the obligation in the Middle Ages, its primary purpose seemed to be that of educating the faithful, particularly converts, in the faith. For by then it was not just a case of the Catholic Christian being bodily present at the celebration of Sunday Mass, but of attentatively hearing the preaching of the Word of God. The Mass had become a teaching tool, and so remains.

For a time, in fact, there were theologians who felt the Sunday obligation extended to presence at evening Vespers, though with only venial or minor sin involved if one was absent. They based their logic on a sunrise to sunset reckoning of the obligation, the principle being that the whole Sunday period was to be kept holy. That opinion has long since been abandoned, and Sunday Vespers is now an observance pretty much confined to monastic and cloister life.

Another shelved custom is that which bound the faithful to hear Sunday Mass in their own parish churches. This custom was introduced with the drawing of parish lines, and was meant to strengthen the parochial system. The policy made the churches of religious orders virtually redundant, however, and members thereof began to preach against the practice late in the thirteenth century. They won their point, but only after "long and severe struggles."

It is obvious from all of this that the church has

always regarded Sunday Mass attendance as a matter of importance. It still does, as Canon 1247 of the new Code of Canon Law makes plain: "On Sundays and Holy Days of Obligation the faithful are bound to participate in the Mass." But the emphases are quite different. Under the old law, bodily presence was what was required; under the new, people are invited to participate in the Mass. The church in effect isn't pounding at consciences and threatening eternal damnation. A new spirit obtains. It presents Sunday as a holy opportunity—a natural and normal part of Christian life, as Father Hans Küng phrases it. One goes to Sunday Mass, not out of obligation or out of fear of being shot down for all eternity by a legalism, but because Sunday Mass is a privilege, a comfort and a joy—or should be, if the liturgy is done right and the sermon is carefully prepared.

As for the holydays, for growing numbers of Catholics they are less and less of a problem of conscience. One can understand why. The number of holydays varies from country to country—the United States has six, France four, Easter Rite churches as many as twenty-eight. Some holydays are purely of local interest—Ireland observes the feast of Saint Patrick as a holyday, Scotland that of Saint Andrew. Holyday observances can be conveniently shifted to Sunday, so that attendance at one Mass then satisfies a double obligation; e.g., in the United States the holydays of

145

John Deedy

Saint Joseph and Saints Peter and Paul are both moved to Sundays. Holyday feasts can be dispensed with by episcopal fiat when they fall on a Saturday or a Monday, thus conflicting with the Sunday obligation and causing problems of a pastoral and practical kind, as for priests ministering to communities miles separated from one another. Finally, holydays are periodically a subject of debate among the bishops themselves, as was demonstrated at the November 1991 annual meeting of the National Conference of Catholic Bishops of the United States, when efforts to reduce the number of holydays in the country failed. Among many Catholics the question therefore arises: How can an issue that is so variable across Christendom and so open to debate within national hierarchies, be so arbitrarily pronounced upon in terms of obligatory Mass attendance and the individual Catholic conscience? The answer is that it can't, certainly not persuasively so.

* * *

The holyday problem begins with the very first feast of the calendar year, January 1.

NOT REALLY . . . The January 1 holyday is something of a problem, but one that exists entirely apart from any associated with the other five holydays of obligation observed in the American church (Christmas, December 25; the Ascension, forty days after Easter;

the Assumption, August 15; All Saints, November 1; and the Immaculate Conception, December 8).

The major difficulty with the latter five holydays—apart from Christmas, that is, a national holiday—is that they can and indeed do commonly fall on a work day, and consequently are observed more in the breach than the observance by the faithful. Because of the likelihood of the holydays coinciding with work days, sentiment has existed for the transferral of their observance to Sundays (as with the holydays of Saint Joseph and Saints Peter and Paul, as noted in the previous entry). The U.S. bishops debated the possibility in 1992, and the proposal received a majority vote, though not the two-thirds necessary for ratification. The full set of holydays thus remains on the books.

The January 1 holyday, on the other hand, is a problem not because of work schedules; like Christmas, January 1 is of course a national holiday, New Year's Day. It is a problem because it is simply an awkward feast that the church hardly seems to know what to do with.

Older Catholics remember January 1 as the Feast of the Circumcision, the eighth day after Christmas, when the foreskin of the penis of the child Jesus was removed in a ritual commemorating the Old Testament's Covenant of God with Abraham. The feast was solemnly observed in Christendom after the sixth century, but somehow it seemed culturally removed from the faith,

147

especially given the earlier rejection of circumcision as a religious obligation for Catholics by the Council of Jerusalem. Thus such paradoxes as to be found in the old Latin Mass for the feast day, where there was no mention of the circumcision except for the passing reference in the gospel of the day: "At that time, after eight days were accomplished that the child should be circumcised. . . " (Luke 2:21). The prayers of the Mass—introit, gradual, offertory, secret, etc.—and the office of the Mass as well were a continuation of the Christmas feast.

Over time the circumcision reference was quietly dropped from the feast's title, as if it were a kind of anatomical embarrassment to Catholic, Jansenist-like sensibilities. The feast was referred to simply as the Octave of Christmas.

But the Octave of Christmas proved too vague a title, and besides it meant nothing devotionally. So in the 1969 reform of the liturgical calendar something else was tried. The January 1 feast was renamed the Solemnity of Mary, Mother of God, thus shifting the feast's emphasis entirely from Jesus to Mary. The shift wasn't entirely inventive; the emphasis was in accordance with Eastern tradition. To provide for liturgical continuum, the new feast was designated by Rome to supplant the former feast of the Maternity of Mary, which had been observed on October 11.

So Solemnity of Mary, Mother of God, the January

Facts, Myths and Maybes

1 holyday is—though the name is often telescoped to Solemnity of Mary. The feast's new name eliminates the liturgical awkwardness of the old Feast of the Circumcision, but Solemnity of Mary, Mother of God? As has been remarked, that designation has the ring of a committee anxious to break for lunch.

* * *

Catholic veneration of the saints borders on idolatry.

NOT SO, or at least it shouldn't . . . It is true that the reformers thought the place of saints in Catholic devotional life to be excessive, and consequently they jettisoned saints throughout Protestantism. This wasn't exactly a case of throwing the baby out with the bath water, for excesses certainly existed, then and later.

Even into the twentieth century Catholic sources were cautioning against abuses in the honoring of saints. In its entry on "Patron Saints," for instance, the 1913 *Catholic Encyclopedia* spoke of "spells and incantations [being] intruded in the place of trust and prayer; the prayerful abstinence of a vigil [being] exchanged for the rollicksome enjoyment of wakes; reverence [running] incidentally to puerile extravagance; and patrons being chosen before their claim to an heroic exercise of Christian virtue had been juridically established."

That the problem did not go away was made evident

John Deedy

by Vatican II and its urging that "all concerned . . . work hard to prevent or correct any abuses, excesses, or defects which may have crept in here or there, and to restore all things to a more ample praise of Christ and of God" (Dogmatic Constitution on the Church, *Lumen gentium*, 51).

Throughout history the church encouraged the cult of the saints; it still does. But if Catholics at times and in places were carried away by excessive enthusiasm, it wasn't official teaching that was at fault. The point might have gotten lost in the fine print, but the letter of church law always had it that adoration belonged only to God. *Latria*, it was called—the supreme worship. Saints were not to be worshipped; rather they were to be honored, venerated, and this the church called *dulia*, from the medieval Latin word for service or work done. In the secular realm, it would be comparable to honoring or venerating a distinguished person for particular works or services.

The distortion of the saints' accurate place in Catholic devotional life stemmed from the fact that as heroes of Christianity saints qualified not only as role models for those who hoped to emulate their holy and heroic virtues, but more particularly as intercessors before the throne of God in the matter of prayerful petitions. The latter circumstance contributed to the popularity of novenas and devotional exercises to saints, and that popularity became so strong and the cult of the saints so dominant among many Catholics as often to eclipse the liturgy and shroud the preeminent place of God the Father, God the Son and the Holy Spirit in Catholic devotional life. It was this distortion that Vatican II sought to correct.

So, yes, abuses existed in the past, and to the extent that they were tolerated that was wrong. For that toleration translated to idolatry or near idolatry in the veneration of saints.

All that seems to belong to the past, however. The reforms of Vatican II and the changed devotional habits of Catholics have put the saints in their place—their proper place, one might add.

* * *

Actually, it was with Rome itself, not with the people in the pews, that the demythologizing of saints originated.

FACT . . . and if the process can be said to have a date of origin, it was April 18, 1961, when the Congregation of Rites dropped Philomena's name from the list of saints for lack of evidence that there ever was a Philomena. Seems the inscription on a tomb discovered in 1802 in Rome's cemetery of Saint Priscilla was misread. *Lumena—Paxte—Cum Fi* was reconstructed to read *Pax—Tecum—Filumena*, ''Peace be with you, Philomena.'' When a phial thought to contain blood was found near the bones, sanctity became added to identity. The parish priest of Mugnano del Cardinale, Dom Francesco di Lucia, sat down and wrote an elaborate account of a third-century virgin martyr based on dubious visions and a pious imagination; her name was Philomena. She was sheer invention. When scholars discovered this, the name was struck from the rolls, although for convenience's sake churches and shrines named for Philomena were allowed to remain on the books.

However, the great revision of the rolls of the saints occurred with Vatican II and the instruction of the Constitution of the Sacred Liturgy, *Sacrosanctum concilium*: "Lest the feasts of the saints should take precedence over the feasts which commemorate the very mysteries of salvation, many of them should be left to be celebrated by a particular church or nation or family of religious; only those should be extended to the universal church which commemorate saints who are truly of universal importance" (111).

That instruction led to a 1969 revision of the Roman Calendar ratified by the *motu proprio* of Paul VI (1963-1978), *Mysterii parchalis celebrationem*. Some thirty saints of dubious authenticity or questionable merit were struck from the calendar, among them some of the earliest and best known. Bye, bye Christopher and Valentine, Ursula and her band of 11,000 virgins, Pudentiana, Modestus, Canute, Susanna, Alexius, and company.

Facts, Myths and Maybes

The office of Devil's Advocate is central to the church's beatification and canonization processes.

NO MORE . . . if indeed it ever was. The name arrests attention, and the imagery is colorful, but the reality is that the Devil's Advocate, *Advocatus Diaboli,* was a rather late addition to the beatification and canonization processes. Admittedly, once introduced, the Devil's Advocate role was anything but insignificant. He functioned as so-called promoter of the faith—in fact, that was his official title, Promoter of the Faith, *Promoter Fidei.* His duty was to present *animadversiones;* that is, to raise objections testing the solidarity of the petitioners' case. But, as said, this development came late in the game of saint-making. By now the church was in its sixteenth century.

Mention of a Devil's Advocate is not found until the pontificate of Leo X (1513-1521), when the office was combined with that of fiscal advocate. It did not become an office of its own until the pontificate of Clement XI (1700-1721). In any case, that's mostly academic. The function of Devil's Advocate was eliminated with the beatification/canonization reforms of 1983 spelled out by John Paul II in the apostolic constitution, *Divinus perfectionis Magister.* A new name was given the Promoter of the Faith. He was now Prelate Theologian, and as Kenneth Woodward wrote in *Making Saints* (Simon & Schuster, 1990), he was assigned "the largely

153

administrative task of choosing the theologicial con-
sultors for each cause and presiding at their meetings.''

The responsibility for demonstrating the validity of
a candidate's cause now belongs to a ''college of rela-
tors,'' whose job is to prepare a historical-critical paper
on the candidate's life, virtues and, where applicable,
martyrdom. Hearings are still to be held, and witnesses
called. But as Woodward noted, the chief sources of
information are to be historical, the principal one being a carefully documented critical biography.

* * *

The distinction between saints and blesseds, the canonized
and the beatified, has increasingly become a blurred one.

FACT . . . The observation is made in the Woodward
book cited in the previous item, *Making Saints*. Woodward argues that ''the division between beatification
and canonization has become a theological distinction
with little practical significance,'' not only because the
requirements for the honors are virtually interchange-
able, but also because the church's crowded liturgical
calendar leaves little room for observing the feastdays
of the multiplied (and multiplying) number of saints
and blesseds.

More than two-thirds of the liturgical calendar is
slotted for events in the life of Christ, the church and

the Virgin Mary. This leaves only about one hundred days open for honoring others. Take away classic feast-days, like those honoring Saint Patrick and Saints Peter and Paul, and there isn't much room left. This means that newly canonized saints are rarely included in liturgical calendars outside their own countries—which in effect relegates them to the status of blesseds, whose cult is observed regionally or locally.

But this is the way it was in the beginning.

Historically, the difference between beatification and canonization was, on the one hand, that of local (or restricted) veneration of one whose life was marked by holiness—these were the blesseds of the beatification process; and on the other hand, universal (or unrestricted) veneration for those whose holiness was certified a second time—these were the canonized or saints of step two in the process. The requirements for elevation were (and remain) essentially the same for both steps.

In the beginning, however, there was no distinction between canonization and beatification. There was no preliminary step to sainthood. Saints were raised up, commonly by local authority and sometimes with great speed, testimonies being gathered on the spot from those acquainted with the individual, with decisions being reached in a matter of weeks and months. Saint Peter of Castelnau, for instance, died January 15, 1208, and was declared a saint the following March 12; Saint Anthony of Padua died June 13, 1231 and was canonized June 3, 1232.

Change came to the business of making saints with the new millennium and the centralizing movement, which gathered to Rome and reserved to the pope the most important ecclesiastical acts and decisions. Alexander III (1159-1181) began the process, but it actually was not completed until the seventeenth century and the reign of Urban VIII (1623-1644).

Urban claimed exclusively for Rome the rights of saint-making, and with decrees in 1625 and 1634 he separated beatification and canonization into ceremonies completely distinct one from the other. Hitherto there was no marked difference between the two. Now, canonization signified a plentitude of honors deserving of recognition throughout the universal church; beatification, a step to that exalted honor, authorized a restricted or local *cultus.* The canonized saint could be venerated everywhere in the church; the beatified blessed had to settle for veneration in a region or country.

So it was, and so it becomes once again, for the reasons mentioned by Woodward.

*   *   *

Pope John Paul II has been one of the busiest beatifiers and canonizers of church history.

Facts, Myths and Maybes

FACT . . . Certainly he has been the busiest of this century. In fact, no other twentieth-century pope is even close. In his nineteen year reign, Pius XII (1939-1958) conducted twenty-three beatification and thirty-three canonization ceremonies. Paul VI (1963-1978) held thirty-one and twenty-one, respectively. Through his first eleven years as pope, John Paul II has presided over one hundred and twenty-three beatifications and twenty-three canonizations.

Moreover to the point, many of John Paul's elevations have involved group causes; e.g., the 117 Vietnamese martyrs of the eighteenth and nineteenth centuries, and the 103 Korean martyrs of the last century. These group ceremonies swell John Paul's total to more than 255 new saints and more than 310 new blesseds.

In fact, so numerous have John Paul's beatifications and canonizations become (almost every foreign trip includes at least one such ceremony, and there are four trips on the average each year) that doubts have been expressed about the policy. In 1989, the secretary of the Congregation for the Causes of Saints, Archbishop Traian Crisan declared, ''We need to be careful. Like anything that is done every day, it loses its value.'' Earlier, Joseph Cardinal Ratzinger of the Congregation of the Doctrine of the Faith remarked on the swelling numbers of saints and blesseds, commenting there were some ''who perhaps mean something to a certain group of people, but do not mean a great deal to the great multitude of believers.''

If any of this was meant to encourage Pope John Paul to slow down and be more selective, it has been without noticeable effect. The ceremonies continue as frequent as ever.

* * *

Indulgences are like double-value food coupons.

NOT QUITE . . . although once upon a time, they certainly were. A vast theology surrounded indulgences, their types (partial, plenary), source (treasury of the church), applications (to the living and the dead), conditions for efficacy (state of grace, confession, communion, etc.), availability (through prayers, deeds, religious objects, etc.), frequency of merit (whether restricted or *toties quoties*, open-ended), and value in terms of time (thirty days, seven years, five quarantines, etc.) The time element was especially worth noting, particularly back when it was thought that even a forgiven sin required the equivalent of seven years' suffering in Purgatory. Frederick the Wise, the pious elector of Saxony, kept track of his indulgences, and over just one twelve-month period calculated that he had accumulated a grand total of 127,999 years' worth of indulgences. To be sure Frederick lived in the thirteenth century, and many of the old Catholic presumptions from that so-called greatest of centuries came to be routed. Yet, as any pre-Vatican II missal will show, indulgences were still being measured in time frames well into our twentieth century.

By the time Vatican II came along, there was considerable sentiment for the dropping entirely of the function of indulgences. That did not happen. Vatican II actually had little or nothing to say on the subject, but a mood had been set, and in 1967 Paul VI issued an apostolic constitution, "The Doctrine of Indulgences," which virtually was a complete restatement of what indulgences were all about. Gone entirely was the "treasury of the church" notion. Gone, too, were the precise, descriptive time frames for indulgences. Instead, the document spoke more vaguely, like " . . . the faithful who perform an action to which a 'partial indulgence' is attached, obtain, in addition to the remission of the temporal punishment acquired by the action itself, an equal remission of punishment through the intervention of the church"—not exactly a double-value coupon, but as the *New Catholic Encyclopedia* whimsically suggests, something like "a matching grant."

In 1968 there was more change, when the Vatican replaced the *Raccolta,* the collection of prayers and pious exercises to which popes had attached indulgences, with an *Enchiridion Indulgentiarum,* "Handbook of Indulgences." The new *Enchiridion* was dramatically shorter than the old manual, and the emphases quite different. ''In conformity with the changed conditions of the present times,'' the *Enchiridion* placed ''greater value . . . one the . . . *opus operantis* [personal contribution] of the faithful . . . instead of [on] a lengthy series of indulgenced works of piety'' [*opus operantum*]. In other words, the disposition of the individual took precedent over the mere performance of an act.

The *Enchiridion* accredited three ''General Grants of Indulgences,'' and listed some seventy grants of indulgences for devotional acts and exercises, such as visits to designated churches or shrines.

Stressed now, however, was not the beefing-up of one's personal treasury of indulgences by the ritualistic fulfillment of some prescribed formula—Frederick the Wise may not have been so sage after all—but instead the spirit of joyful and efficacious participation in the fellowship or communion of the saints and the prayer life of the church. Fair enough.

* * *

If Catholic veneration of saints isn't idolatrous, most certainly Catholic veneration of images must be.

NOT SO, AGAIN . . . This is an issue, though, that bedeviled the church in the eighth and ninth centuries; which involved cruel persecutions; which was addressed by general councils, and which some think

Facts, Myths and Maybes

was settled in part as a matter of accommodation—
the East-West schism being threatened, and the West
not being anxious to antagonize the image-conscious
East on yet another matter of mutual concern.

The point of issue, quite simply, was whether the
veneration of images was in violation of the First Commandment: "I am the Lord thy God . . . Thou shalt
have no other gods before me. Thou shalt not make
unto thee any graven image, or any likeness of any
thing that is in heaven above, or that is in the earth
beneath, or that is in water under the earth. Thou shalt
not bow down thyself to them, nor serve them: for
I the Lord am a jealous God . . . " (Exodus 20:2-5).

The Eastern church saw nothing wrong with images,
and profusely adorned its places of worship with icons,
paintings, mosaics and bas-reliefs—though, interestingly enough, not with solid statues, or not many at
least, perhaps because statues smacked too much of
the representations of the Greek gods being left behind
by the general populace.

The Western church, on the other hand, was ambiguous at the time. There were many—bishops included—
who, drawing on Exodus as well as on Jewish and
Moslem precedents, felt that religious images not only
perpetuated a heathen custom, but also encouraged
practices of idolatry. It was generally fine, therefore,
when the Emperor Leo III in 726 declared the veneration of images to be idolatrous, and banned all use of

them on grounds they were a hindrance to the conversion of Jews and Muslims. A wholesale destruction of priceless works of art followed. Defenders of images, such as Germanus, Patriarch of Constantinople, were deposed and/or persecuted. Iconoclasts—''image breakers,'' in the Greek—were in the ascendancy, and continued so during the reign of the Emperor Constantine V (741-775). In one month alone in the year 766, sixteen high officials and army officers were executed for defending the use and veneration of relics.

The images' issue grew into an East-West flash point, the East being particularly sensitive on the subject because of the special place of religious art and objects in Eastern churches and in the Eastern liturgy itself.

The issue was dealt with at the Council of Nicaea in 787. Synodal decrees ordering suppression of religious images were abrogated, and Iconoclasm, the doctrines of iconoclasts, was declared a heresy as real as Arianism, the fourth-century teaching that denied the divinity of Christ. Said Nicaea: ''Pictorial representations of Christ, of the Mother of God, the Angels and the Saints, are lawful, for by this means the beholder is put in mind of their prototypes and encouraged to imitate them. The cult paid to images is related to the prototype and is distinct from the adoration which is due to God alone.'' Nicaea's word was definitive; nothing has been added or subtracted since.

Iconoclasm did not disappear immediately, of course,

but policy had been set. Images belonged. To Gregory the Great (590-604) they were to the illiterate what books were to those who could read—or, as he said to one iconoclast bishop, Serenus of Marseilles, ''In a picture even the unlearned may see what example they should follow; in a picture they who know no letters may yet read; hence for barbarians especially, a picture takes the place of a book.''

Of course, then as now excesses must be protected against.

One final note, with the settling of the iconoclast controversy, prostrations, kissing, incensing, bowing to the cross, etc., became fully accepted gestures and ways of expressing respect and honor. In Catholic logic, they are equivalent in the secular realm to a saluting of the flag—nothing less, nothing more.

* * *

Angels are a large part of biblical history, and also of the continuing Catholic consciousness.

HALF TRUE . . . Biblical history is indeed replete with stories of angels. In the Old Testament, for instance, there's the angel who found Hagar by a spring in the wilderness (Genesis 16); the angels of the Sodom and Gomorrah narrative (Genesis 19); the angel who announced to Gideon that he was to save his people (Judges 6:11-18); the angel who instructed Daniel on the vision of the ram and the goat (Daniel 8:15-27), etc. In the New Testament there's the angel of Mary's annunciation (Luke 1:26-38); the angel who reassured Joseph about Mary's pregnancy (Matthew 1:20-21); the angel who announced Christ's Resurrection to Mary Magdalene and the other Mary (Matthew 28:2-7), etc.

But the history of angels isn't confined to the Bible. There's also tradition. So prominent were angels in the Catholic psyche that Saint Jerome proposed that everyone had his or her own angel from birth. "The dignity of a soul is [that] great," he argued. The idea took root, and with it the concept of guardian angels. The existence of guardian angels was never defined as dogma by the church, but they were accorded a universal feast in 1608 by Pope Paul V (1605-1621). That Feast of the Guardian Angels belongs still to the liturgical calendar, being observed on October 2.

For many Catholics, however, the notion of angels today belongs more to symbolic imagery than theological reality. They're no big deal. Saint Thomas Aquinas devoted 126 pages of the *Summa Theologica* (Random House edition, 1945) to the subject of angels. The *New Catholic Encyclopedia* (1967) was much, much briefer, and actually a mite cautionary. Two "extremes" are to be avoided in evaluating accounts of angels taken from the Bible and Catholic tradition reads its entry: "On the one hand, not everything that is therein contained can be taken as fact, because much of it belongs simply to the philosophy of life in antiquity and must be discarded; so, too, the existence and efficacy of angels cannot be denied out of hand simply because it is possible today, because of more accurate knowledge, to explain by natural causes what was once attributed to angels.''

As for the actual existence of angels, the *New Catholic Encyclopedia*'s entry more or less winds up begging the question. ''The believing Christian . . . will even today maintain that there are angels because the Bible and the church teach it,'' the *Encyclopedia* declares. ''. . . One knows that angels exist, as Saint Augustine once said, through faith [*esse angelos novimus ex fide*].''

The modern mind, however, tends toward skepticism. Rightly or wrongly, it considers angels ''to be tenuous creatures who, with the passage of time, are more and more being relegated to the sphere of legend, fairy tale, and child's fancy.'' Why the quotes? Those words, too, are from the *New Catholic Encyclopedia*.

* * *

If the existence of angels is doubtful for many people, it follows that so also is the existence of Satan or the Devil.

NOT NECESSARILY . . . Norman Mailer, in a 1992 interview with TV's David Frost, conceded that when one talks of Satan or the Devil one gets strange looks from folks, almost as if one were ''off the wall,'' to use his phrase. On the other hand, how else does one account for the reality of evil in the world? The Sunday homilist advises that the most incomprehensible of evils, such as the heart-wrenching illness of a child or inopportune death of a young parent, may actually be part of God's plan—that out of these seeming evils a good results, one that individuals might not even recognize. A pious thought. But then how could a God who is infinitely good and all powerful allow something so montrous as the Holocaust? That's what Norman Mailer wants to know, and he's not alone in asking that question. The Holocaust is a problem for Christians as well as for Jewish people.

Mailer's rationale is that ours is an "imperfect God," and that the Holocaust was a most dramatic instance of the Devil's triumph over "him"—or "her," as the case may be . . . the gender distinction entered by Mailer.

The suggestion may be unsatisfactory. An imperfect God? But have Catholic theologians a better explanation for the impassivity of an all-loving, all-powerful God in the face of so unmitigated an evil? Could the Holocaust have been the Devil's triumph, as Mailer speculated? How could it have been? Theoretically the Devil was overcome eons ago. The Lord himself said that he "watched Satan fall from the sky like lightning" (Luke 10:18), and the disciples themselves rejoiced that ''even the demons were subject'' to them in God's name (Luke 10:17).

Satan may have been conquered, but evil has persisted—and with disorders so large and so often so far beyond human comprehension and the seeming capacity of individuals for evil that the disorders can only be accounted for in terms of a force such as Satan or the Devil. Is this Catholic fantasy at work? Hardly. Martin Luther was also convinced that Satan hovered near, ever the Great Tempter—and, of course, evil doer.

So evils continued, and then there was the Holocaust, the ultimate evil. Does one lay it to the Devil or Satan? There's no answer. As Passionist Father Carroll Stuhlmueller once observed, the degree of evil in the world manifests the limits of theology. So does the Holocaust.

* * *

The church has eliminated the old obligation known as the Easter Duty.

NOT SO . . . For a variety of reasons, Catholics are not dunned from the altar about the Easter Duty obligation, as so often was the case in the past. But the obligation is still very much on the books, although with time-span broadened. ''For a good reason'' the Easter

John Deedy

Duty, so called, may now be fulfilled not just in the Eastertide (the period extending from the first Sunday of Lent to Trinity Sunday), but anytime during the year. This is the way Canon 920, sections 1 and 2, of the new Code of Canon Law phrases the obligation: "Once admitted to the blessed Eucharist, each of the faithful is obliged to receive holy communion at least once a year. This precept must be fulfilled during paschal time, unless for a good reason it is fulfilled at another time during the year."

The requirement then is a serious one. At the same time it is one which the church regards as minimal in complying with the divine injunction to partake of the body and blood of Christ, and preserve the life of grace in the individual soul. In other words, Catholics are actually expected to receive communion more often than once a year.

The Easter Duty obligation was promulgated by Lateran Council IV (1215), and it eased an earlier prescript which made it obligatory for Catholics to receive communion three times a year (Christmas, Easter and Pentecost). The Council of Trent (1545-1563) repeated the obligation of receiving during the Easter season.

Paradoxically, one result of the old emphasis on annual reception of the Eucharist was to reduce its reception during the rest of the year. That once-a-year emphasis fostered in many individuals a rigorism about penitential disposition and a feeling of unworthiness about receiving the sacrament on a more frequent basis. The condition was widespread and persisted into the twentieth century before being rooted out by Pope Pius X (1903-1914), who became known in the process as the pope of frequent communion. Pius X encouraged frequent communion by requiring but two conditions for its reception: state of grace and pious intention.

Today, with more relaxed penitential dispositions and eased fast and abstinence regulations, communion is received by almost everyone attending the ceremony of the Mass—another reason no doubt why reminders from the altar about Easter Duty are unnecessary. Regular reception of the sacrament by the people in the pews has made the reminders redundant.

One effect of the new practice has been to end controversy over whether confession (now the sacrament of reconciliation) was a necessary part of the Easter Duty obligation. It isn't, and indeed never was. Canon Law 989 states: "All the faithful who have reached the age of discretion are bound faithfully to confess their grave sins at least once a year." Since it is not necessary to confess minor or venial sins, it follows from the modifier "grave" in Canon 989 that one is not in fact obliged to confess once a year. The canon would seem to apply only to those who had committed "grave" sin. The church, however, does encourage periodic use

169

of the sacrament by all. The problem for the church, as noted earlier, is that the encouragement falls on deaf ears.

* * *

Like the Ten Commandments, the fourteen Stations of the Cross are etched in stone—or, as the case may be, plaster of Paris.

ANYTHING BUT . . . The Stations or Way of the Cross *(Via Crucis)* is a devotion of Middle-Ages origin, developing under Franciscan impetus in the twelfth and thirteenth centuries as a substitute for pilgrimages to the Holy Land. By moving from station to station, the devout in "little Jerusalems" could vicariously retrace the steps of Jesus as he moved from the palace of Pilate to Calvary and burial, and could do so conveniently and without danger to life and limb that accompanied travel in a distant and hostile Middle East. But it was centuries before the number of stations of this devotion was established as fourteen. Depending on time and place, manuals of devotion gave the number at anywhere from five to thirty-seven.

In fact, it was not until 1731 and the reign of Clement XII (1730-1740) that the general features of the devotion were agreed upon and that the number was fixed as fourteen. Principal influences were Belgian and German Catholics and their methods for saying the Stations. Presumably, the devotional ways at Louvain and Nuremberg were more striking than those at Jerusalem. In any case, with the fixing of the number at fourteen, gone forever were many stations of dubious authenticity or only tangentially associated with Christ's way to Calvary, among them the house of Dives, the Blessed Virgin's school, the city gate through which Christ passed, the probatic pool, the houses of Herod and Simon the Pharisee, etc.

Still, the Stations of the Cross were not indelibly cast in 1731. In the 1960s, it became practice in some places to add a fifteenth station representing the Resurrection, and at the 1991 Good Friday service in Rome's Colosseum, Pope John Paul II introduced an extensive revision of the Stations, though still keeping the total number at fourteen.

John Paul's revisions are better grasped by first reviewing the traditional fourteen in place after the sixteenth century. They were titled: (1) Jesus is condemned to death; (2) Jesus takes up his cross; (3) Jesus falls the first time; (4) Jesus meets his afflicted mother; (5) Simon of Cyrene helps Jesus; (6) Veronica wipes the face of Jesus; (7) Jesus falls the second time; (8) Jesus comforts the women of Jerusalem; (9) Jesus falls the third time; (10) Jesus is stripped of his garments; (11) Jesus is nailed to the cross; (12) Jesus dies on the cross; (13) Jesus is taken down from the cross; (14) Jesus is laid in the tomb.

John Deedy

What John Paul did was eliminate all stations not mentioned in the New Testament. Dropped therefore were Veronica wiping the face of Jesus, the three falls of Jesus, and, perhaps most surprising of all, the meeting of Jesus with his afflicted mother. All, it develops, were pious inventions of history. The story of Veronica, for instance, seems rooted in Luke's reference to the company of women who "bewailed and lamented" Jesus as he carried his cross to Calvary (23:27). Devout presumption was that one of the women wiped blood from his face, and in gratitude Jesus left his true image (*vera icon*) on the cloth; hence came the name Veronica and an account of alleged compassion.

With John Paul's revision, the Stations of the Cross are titled: (1) The agony in the garden; (2) Jesus, betrayed by Judas, is arrested; (3) Jesus is condemned by the Sanhedrin; (4) Jesus is denied by Peter; (5) Jesus is judged by Pilate; (6) Jesus is scourged and crowned with thorns; (7) Jesus takes up his cross; (8) Jesus is helped by Simon of Cyrene to carry his cross; (9) Jesus meets the women of Jerusalem; (10) Jesus is crucified; (11) Jesus promises redemption to the good thief; (12) Jesus on the cross, with his mother and Saint John at the foot of the cross; (13) Jesus dies on the cross; (14) Jesus is placed in the tomb.

Is John Paul's the last word on the stations? Probably not. Vatican Master of Ceremonies Monsignor

Facts, Myths and Maybes

Piero Marini said the old Stations of the Cross remain "fully valid and may be taken up again in the future." Later, lest pastors rush out and start remodeling their churches, Vatican authorities reiterated that the old way is still acceptable, and that the new form was created as an alternative. Of course further revisions are possible. The Stations of the Cross do not belong to dogma. There's nothing immutable about them.

What finally of Pope John Paul's stations?

"The 1991 Way of the Cross spotlights the tragic play of personalities, the struggle between light and darkness, between the truth and falsehood which they incarnate," said Marini. The new Stations encourage Christians "to cry over our sin as did Peter; to become open to Jesus, the suffering Messiah, as did the good thief; to remain close to the cross of Christ, as did his mother and disciple; and to gather with them the word that saves, the blood that purifies, the spirit which gives life."

That's very moving.

The trouble is that with the eclipse of devotional Catholicism, hardly anyone says the Stations of the Cross anymore.

*   *   *

New liturgical emphases have virtually eliminated black from the church's color charts.

John Deedy

FACT . . . Traditionally black was the liturgical color of mourning, and it was used for funerals, Masses for the dead, and the ceremonies of Good Friday. It has not been completely eliminated as one of the five basic liturgical colors, but with the reforms of Vatican Council II (1962-1965) it has largely been displaced. The color for funeral Masses, for instance, now is generally white, symbolic of the resurrection, while the color for Good Friday is red, symbolic of martyrdom, Christ being the prototype of all martyrs.

Until the fourth century there was only one liturgical color—white. Other colors were gradually introduced, and grew to importance in the Middle Ages as the liturgy was shaped to play more and more on the five senses; e.g., incense on smell; music on hearing; color and pageantry on sight, etc. The basic colors came to be standardized after the Council of Trent (1545-1563). In addition to white, they were red, green, violet (or purple) and black, with off-shades (rose, blue) being allowed for special occasions.

Priests frequently vest in gold for solemn rites, but strictly speaking gold is not a liturgical color.

The liturgical colors and their symbolism:

White: the color of purity and joy. It is the color of Christmas and Easter, as well as the feasts and com-memorations of the Blessed Virgin, angels, saints who are not martyrs, All Saints and specified feasts. It can be substituted for other colors, including, as mentioned, for requiems and offices of the dead.

Black: once again, the color of mourning, but seldom used anymore, as the church prefers instead to emphasize themes of joy and blessed anticipation.

Violet (or purple): this is now the dominant pentitential color. It is used mainly during Advent and Lent.

Green: the color of hope and growth, used most frequently from mid-January to the eve of Septuagesima Sunday, and after Trinity Sunday until the eve of the first Sunday of Advent. It is the principal color of the liturgical period known as Ordinary Time, so called because no major feasts distract or intrude upon the special character of the Sunday liturgy.

Red: the color of fire and blood. It is used on the feasts of the Apostles and martyrs, as well as feasts connected with the passion and death of Christ, including Pentecost and, as said, Good Friday.

The shade rose is the color of joy anticipated, and is used in place of purple, or violet, on such feasts as Gaudete Sunday (third Sunday of Advent) and Laetare Sunday (fourth Sunday of Lent). Blue is used mostly in Spain, and then for Marian feasts. Yellow, commonly used between the twelfth and sixteenth centuries, has been retired.

John Deedy

Vatican II's Declaration on Religious Freedom was superfluous, as the church had long since come to an implicit acceptance of the principle of religious liberty.

MYTH . . . True, the church had long since stopped burning heretics. And true, as the so-called Boston Heresy Case of the 1940s involving Father Leonard Feeney made clear, the church was moving away from the proposition that error had no rights and was entitled to no tolerance.

Nonetheless, pre-Vatican II Catholic source books, such as Bishop LaRavoire Morrow's *My Catholic Faith* (My Mission House, 1936, 1961), still carried statements like, "If there is no freedom of thought in mathematics, why in religion?" And more significantly, the Gilmary Society's *Catholic Encyclopedia* (1913, copyright renewed 1940), the standard reference tool on things Catholic right up to the Council, was stating in its entry on "Toleration": "A person who is tolerant in the domain of dogma resembles the botanist who cultivates in his experimental beds both edible plants and poisonous herbs as alike valuable growths, while a person intolerant of error may be compared to a market-gardener, who allows only edible plants to grow, and eradicates noxious weeds. Just as vice possesss no real right to exist, whatever toleration may be shown to the vicious person, so also religious error can lay no just claim to forbearance and indulgence, even though the erring person may merit the greatest affection and esteem.''

In addition, on official levels the church was still committed, or at least had not repudiated, the 1864 Syllabus of Errors of Pius IX nor Pius X's 1907 condemnation of Modernism. The two documents stood as bulwarks against what was regarded as indifferentism, theological dilution, secularism and other unearthly evils. As such the documents were a defense of traditional rights of the church and of ''truth'' against what was viewed as abuses of freedom and of culture.

So, of course, the entire topic of religious freedom needed review by the time Vatican II came along. Nothing less was possible if the church was to seem something more than an insular, Dark Ages institution.

What then would be the subject matter, the issue, opening the doors for the review that would bring the church abreast of developments in the modern world, and to an acceptance of the idea that God might indeed work through other churches than just the Catholic? The issue proved to be that of church and state.

Enter Father John Courtney Murray, American Jesuit and principal architect of *Dignitatis Humanae*, the Declaration on Religious Freedom, the Council document that enunciated new church emphases on religious freedom and the dignity of the individual as a human and religious right, personal and collective.

John Deedy

The very opening words of the document contained the substance of thought that would set the church on new courses of tolerance and of ecumenical understanding and cooperation. Those words: ''A sense of the dignity of the human person has been impressing itself more and more deeply on the consciousness of contemporary man. And the demand is increasingly made that men should act on their own judgment, enjoying and making use of a responsible freedom, not driven by coercion, but motivated by a sense of duty'' (1).

No one Council document placed the church more squarely in the modern, pluralistic world.

* * *

Vatican Council II specifically repudiated the old Christian libel of ''Deicide,'' or ''Killer of God,'' that had been leveled against the Jews of Christ's time, and that had carried across the centuries—by implication rather than through formal teaching—as a source of anti-semitism.

TRUE . . . The Council's Declaration on the Relationship of the Church to Non-Christians, *Nostra aetate,* officially promulgated by Paul VI, said: ''True, authorities of the Jews and those who followed their lead pressed for the death of Christ (cf. John 19:6); still, what happened in his passion cannot be blamed upon all Jews then living, without distinction, nor upon the Jews of

Facts, Myths and Maybes

today. Although the church is the new people of God, the Jews should not be presented as repudiated or cursed by God, as if such views followed from the Holy Scriptures. All should take pains, then, lest in catechetical instruction and in the preaching of God's Word they teach anything out of harmony with the truth of the Gospel and the spirit of Christ" (4).

The Council's action, widely hailed despite not actually including the phrase "or guilty of deicide" (some Council Fathers felt the phrase ambiguous and worried it might suggest that the church no longer regarded Jesus as God), can be considered a legacy of John XXIII—not only because John convoked the Council, but also because during his short pontificate he set the tone which made the Council's action the more possible.

It was John XXIII who lauded Abraham as "the great partriarch of all believers"; who greeted a delegation of American Jews led by Rabbi Herbert Friedman with the words, "I am your brother"; and who stunned the congregation at a Good Friday liturgy in St. Peter's Basilica by bringing the service to a halt and demanding that the prayer of the church for the Jews be repeated without the objectionable reference to the "perfidity" of the Jews. That prayer: *Oremus et pro perfidis Judaeis: ut Deus et Dominus noster auferat velamen de Cordibus eorum; ut ipsi agnoscant Jesum Christum Dominum nostrum;* "Let us pray, also, for the perfidious

181

Jews, that our Lord and God may take away the veil from their hearts, so that they, too, may acknowledge Jesus Christ our Lord.''

In English translations *perfidis* had been softened to ''faithless'' or ''unbelieving,'' but the church was using Latin then as the language of the liturgy; the slur was blatant. In any instance, paralogisms of whatever sort were not acceptable to John XXIII. *Perfidis* was excised, forever. The Council's action flowed naturally from John XXIII's leads.

* * *

The Declaration on Religious Freedom opened Pandora's box, so to speak, making religious freedom an issue within the church itself.

TRUE . . . The Declaration on Religious Freedom was addressed to the broad family of humankind, rather than to internal Catholicism *per se*. But its impact within Catholicism would prove enormous, as individual Catholics applied the principle of religious freedom to their individual lives, both as Christian believers and practicing Catholics. Thus came to be the momentous expressions of freedom within institutional Catholicism that we know so well—on moral questions, such as sexual morality, divorce, second marriages, etc.; and in areas of discipline, notably among priests and sisters in formal religious life.

Facts, Myths and Maybes

These developments are hardly what the Council Fathers had intended or anticipated. Catholicism had always been such an orderly, self-contained entity, its people so bound by the church's dogmatic code and so responsive to authority, that nobody or at least very, very few—John Courtney Murray among the latter— expected Catholics to appropriate the Council's religious-liberty concept to themselves in their Catholic lives. What the Council Fathers and their heirs discovered, however, was that religious freedom was not an easily controlled, neatly compartmentalized concept, one that could be extended in the one direction and restricted in the other. It applied across the board— that is, to Catholics as well as persons of other faiths.

Murray saw the implications of religious freedom most clearly. "The conciliar affirmation of the principle of freedom was narrowly limited—in the text," Murray wrote immediately after the Council. "But the text itself was flung into a pool whose shores are wide as the universal church. The ripples will run far." How far? "Inevitably, a second great argument will be set afoot—now on the theological meaning of Christian freedom. The children of God will receive this freedom as a gift from their Father through Christ in the Holy Spirit, assert it *within the church* (emphasis added) as well as within the world, always for the sake of the world and the church."

Unfortunately Murray was not around to help resolve

John Deedy

the questions that would be spawned by the Council document. He died in 1967 at the premature age of sixty-three, when the assertions of Christian freedom were just beginning within the church.

As seer, Murray had not fixed on any single religious freedom issue or any set of issues that would engage the church, but he did suggest categories: "the dignity of the Christian, the foundations of Christian freedom, its object or content, its limits and their criterion, the measure of its responsible use, its relation to the legitimate reaches of authority and to the saving counsels of prudence, the perils that lurk in it, and the forms of corruption to which it is prone." [The quotes are from Murray's introduction to the chapter on the Declaration on Religious Freedom in *The Documents of Vatican II*, edited by Walter M. Abbott, S.J. (Guild Press, American Press, Association Press, New York, 1966, pp. 672-674.)]

It is impossible to sum up the religious freedom issue within Catholicism, as the matter is far from having run its full course. But one can sum up on John Courtney Murray, perhaps best by borrowing from Jesuit Father Walter J. Burghardt's eulogy at Murray's funeral Mass: "Unborn millions will never know how much their freedom is tied to this man . . . how much the civilized dialogue they take for granted between Christian and Christian, between Christian and Jew, between Christian and unbeliever is made possible by this man, whose life was a civilized conversation.''

Besides honoring Murray, Burghardt's point underscores the changed situation brought about by the Declaration on Religious Freedom. A quarter-century plus after its promulgation, it might be said that however disorderly, however disedifying the transition from the past, the new reality is worth the trouble, the aggravation and the occasional pain.

* * *

The loftiness of the church's social documents notwithstanding, the church's role in the field of social justice has really been one of catch-up.

TRUE ENOUGH . . . though the church has ''caught-up'' rather remarkably. Still it is true that Catholic social doctrine was not one of its strong cards before Pope Leo XIII (1878-1903) issued *Rerum novarum*—Latin title of the encyclical ''On the Condition of the Working Man.'' That document was issued in 1891, over a century ago—hardly a tick of the clock as the church measures time.

In fact, before *Rerum novarum* the church was not even in the social-action game. Interest was centered more on matters within the sanctuary, and existing ''outside'' concerns of a social kind were generally

185

exceptions to the rule. The church had no social program, and it cost. As Pope Pius XI (1922-1939) would lament to Belgium's Abbe Joseph Cardijn in 1927, the great scandal of the church of the nineteenth century was that it lost the working classes. Pius XI spoke in the context of Europe, but he could have been speaking of a condition that was far worse. For the church's narrowness of vision could easily have cost it the working class in the United States as well as Europe—indeed, very well might well have, had not Baltimore's James Cardinal Gibbons intervened in Rome in 1887 to head off condemnation of the American Knights of Labor, precursor of the organized labor movement in this country.

Rerum novarum signaled a change of attitudes. More than that, *Rerum novarum* was the beginning within Catholicism of a systematized theology of social justice, one expanded on since by several popes, an ecumenical council, a synod of bishops, and at least one national hierarchy. Notable contributions in this theological and social evolution (assist from *Salt* magazine):

Quadragesimo anno, ''On Reconstruction of the Social Order''—Pius XI's 1931 updating of *Rerum novarum* in the context of the Great Depression, the stirrings of communism, and the public's vested interest in just and equitable settlements of labor-management disputes.

Facts, Myths and Maybes

Mater et magistra, "Christianity and Social Progress" —John XXIII's 1961 encyclical updating both *Rerum novarum* and *Quadragesimo anno,* bringing focus on the disparities between the developed and undeveloped world, and warning against the social debilitations of the arms race.

Pacem in terris, "Peace on Earth"—John XXIII's 1963 placement of human rights, the dignity of the individual, and order between peoples in contextual relationship from the level of family to that of international councils, while at the same time entering into social equations issues such as racism, feminism and the arms race.

Gaudium et spes, "The Church in the Modern World" —Vatican II's 1965 pastoral constitution directing the "people of God" to scrutinize the technologies and social forces that are transforming family and world, and to quicken their individual potentials for good by Gospel-oriented involvements in the developments and usages of these technologies and forces.

Populorum progressio, "On the Development of Peoples"—Paul VI's 1967 encyclical on the progress of peoples in their full human potential, and the concomitant need for drastic measures to correct the growing imbalance between rich nations and poor nations.

Octogesima adveniens, "A Call to Action"—Paul VI's 1971 apostolic letter to Canada's Maurice Cardinal Roy

187

focusing on the post-industrial society, and calling attention to the "new poor," including the elderly, the handicapped and society's marginalized peoples.

Iustitia in mundo, "Justice in the World"—The 1971 statement of the Third International Synod of Bishops probing "oppression" and "liberation," cataloguing injustices against migrants and refugees, among them human-rights violations, torture and political imprisonments, and calling on the church to be a witness for justice in the way it treats its own members and employees.

Evangelii nuntiandi, "Evangelization in the Modern World"—Paul VI's 1975 apostolic exhortation to the Fourth International Synod of Bishops linking the church's mission to the liberation of all peoples from oppression, and stressing the importance of evangelization in an increasingly de-Christianized world.

Laborem exercens, "On Human Work"—John Paul II's 1981 encyclical on ideological competition between East and West, on human work, and on the place of labor unions as "an indispensable element" of modern industrial society and a vehicle "for the struggle for social justice."

"Economic Justice for All"—The U.S. bishops' 1986 pastoral letter urging the use of the resources of faith and the American economy to shape a society that better protects the dignity and rights of people everywhere on the globe.

Facts, Myths and Maybes

Sollicitudo rei socialis, ''On Social Concern''—John Paul II's 1988 encyclical on the rivalry between the superpowers, and the debilitating effects of this on Third-World countries in terms of national debts, civilian unemployment, recessions and morale. Among the document's targets: consumerism and waste.

Centesimus annus, ''The Hundredth Year''—John Paul II's 1991 encyclical dealing with questions raised by socio-economic changes in Eastern Europe with the collapse of communism. The document continued the church on a middle course between capitalism and socialism, but broke new ground in citing ''the free market [as] the most efficient instrument for utilizing resources and responding to needs.''

The church does not offer these documents as specific, detailed blueprints for action, but rather as a framework for putting theology and philosophy in the service of social justice. The documents are not immutable, but belong to an on-going system of social analysis. There will be more.

* * *

The just-war theory is alive and well, and living in Catholic theology.

TRUE . . . although theologians are increasingly coming to the opinion that the just-war theory is an anachronism.

John Deedy

The church's moral views on war were given preliminary shape by Augustine, systematized by Thomas Aquinas, and refined by the Spanish Scholastics. The net result was the two-level just-war theory (*jus ad bello* and *jus in bello*) that is invoked to this day, including by the U.S. bishops in their famous 1983 pastoral letter, "The Challenge of Peace: God's Promise and Our Response."

Spelling out the theory. . . .

Jus ad bello, the justification for taking up arms, is predicated on the cause being just. There must be a declaration of war by competent authority; there must be a right intention seeking the restoration of peace; all alternatives must have been exhausted; there must be a probability of success, and an assessment of proportionality—that is, the expectations of good must outweigh the likelihood of the negative or bad effects.

Jus in bello, the actual state of combat, is similarly conditioned. Proportionality again demands that the good outweigh the evil; the safety of noncombatants must be respected; and direct targeting must be restricted to combatants, military installations and factories directly involved in war production, etc.

All this could—and did—work when wars were orderly exercises, fought in the countryside or on the sea with arms of limited potency and limited threat to the wider population. In that setting, the just-war theory worked as a check on violence, and in the face of hostilities, it stood as a reminder of the moral accountability shared by all parties to the violence, real or potential. The question now is whether the just-war theory has any relevance anymore, except perhaps in local or small-scale conflicts, as in wars of liberation from an oppressor. Said another way, has modern weaponry made the just-war theory obsolete?

Many theologians think so. They feel that the just-war theory is not only outmoded, but just plain dead. And it isn't just because of the existence of nuclear weapons, justification for any use of which few attempt with real conviction anymore, whatever the scenario. It is also because conventional weapons are today so awesome and so potentially indiscriminate in their effects as to make mere discussion about a just-war something of an exercise in semantics.

Those rejecting the just-war theory make no exception for the so-called "smart" bombs of modern arsenals. President Bush invoked the just-war theory, and used "smart" bombs in his Persian Gulf war of 1991. For all the patriotic hoopla, the Persian Gulf war was as unjust a war as might be imagined. But then, what else could a war fought out of selfish considerations over oil be except unjust?

* * *

John Deedy

Annulment is more than ever a Catholic code word for divorce.

FOUL! . . . though it may seem so to critics, annulments being so numerous nowadays. In 1968 only 450 annulments were granted by Catholic marriage tribunals in the United States, pretty much the annual average for those times; in 1981 the number was 48,000; in 1986, it was 57,681. In fact, of the 71,352 annulment petitions introduced worldwide in 1988, U.S. Catholics accounted for 72 percent. Obviously, a radical change has taken place, but it still doesn't mean that the church has gone into the divorce business under the cover of annulments.

Today as yesterday, the church holds a valid marriage to be indissoluble. An annulment is its declaration that no sacramental marriage bond had ever existed, because of a lack of validity traceable to an unknown or concealed impediment, an essential defect in consent, or a condition placed by one or both of the parties against the nature of the sacrament. With a decree of nullity, an annulment, the individuals concerned are free to marry with the church's consent.

But if definition has not changed, how come so many more annulments?

First, the process itself has been relaxed, making the procedure much less intimidating for petitioners, much less a test and a trial. Second, new pastoral and psychological understandings have come into play broadening the grounds for annulments.

The old rules were laid down by the Council of Trent in the sixteenth century, and they were tough. Annulments were granted only if one of the parties did not fully consent (e.g., out of fear or coercion), or was unable to fulfill the marital obligation of a spouse (e.g., impotency), or if the proper dispensation had not been given to one of the canonical impediments to a valid marriage (e.g., blood relationship or affinity). Not only were the grounds narrow and rigidly defined, but tribunal hearings were held before an exclusively clerical male court that many going through the process found could be medieval in its attitudes. Horror stories abound.

Now Catholic marriage tribunals are integrated with sisters and laity serving in various capacities and bringing new insights and understandings to the process.

Of equal pertinence, sympathetic consideration is now given to psychological and behavioral factors that could not even have been raised by petitioners just a generation ago. For instance, gross immaturity may now be grounds for annulment, when it can be demonstrated that it affected in a serious way the interpersonal relationships of the couple or the faith aspect of their union. Since gross immaturity could have existed a short or long time ago, the annulment process is opened up not only to young couples, but to persons

193

of older age who might be the parents of fully grown families. Gross immaturity is not a uniquely American nuance, incidentally. In a 1984 address to the Roman Rota, Paul VI cited "grave lack of discretionary judgment" as a deficiency to a valid marriage.

But if the annulment process has been relaxed, other aspects of the church's marriage laws and customs have not. Unacceptable, for example, are so-called "good conscience" second marriages, which some U.S. dioceses were quietly recognizing in the early 1970s, before Rome blew the whistle. Unacceptable too is the proposition that marriages which are emotionally and psychologically dead are dead in fact, thus freeing individuals for another marriage.

By church law, a valid marriage remains a permanent bond, until death do them part, as the saying goes. Civil divorce, by the same token, is a legal arrangement, tolerated by the church out of considerations of family, health, custody of children, property, and the like. But the church is emphatic: civil divorce does not affect the bond of a valid marriage. In the church's eyes, that couple is still married. There can be no new marriage ceremony in the church, without the church's granting of an annulment . . . which again is the declaration that no marriage existed in the first place.

* * *

Facts, Myths and Maybes

The odds favor petitioners in annulment proceedings.

FACT . . . In 1988 (the most recent year, as of mid-1992, for which complete figures were available), determinations in favor of nullity were granted in 96 percent of cases introduced by American Catholics. Rome has expressed concern over this remarkably high percentage figure on more than one occasion, but the fact is that the American percentage is only slightly higher than the worldwide average. In 1988 the worldwide average was 94 percent.

Most annulment decisions, incidentally, are made on the local and regional levels, and it is only when there is lack of concurrence between the hearing tribunal and the review board that a particular case is forwarded on to Rome. Unresolvable cases are not frequent. Between 1980 and 1985, only forty-seven of an estimated 150,000 to 180,000 cases involving U.S. Catholics had to be channeled to Rome.

*　*　*

Abortion is a latter-day preoccupation of the Catholic Church.

FALSE . . . It is true that until recent years the church seemed quiet on the subject of abortion, but that is only because abortion was not the great issue that it is now. There was agreement among virtually all governments and churches that abortion was evil, and this conformance had been in place for centuries. Abortion was proscribed in civil as well as ecclesial law, and those laws were so widely accepted by peoples, that there was about as much need to make an issue of abortion as there was of defending motherhood and the flag.

The fact is that, from its very beginning, Catholic Christianity was unequivocally opposed to abortion and committed to the defense of unborn—and the newborn. The commitment was urgent at the dawn of Christianity, for not only was the fetus regularly under attack, but also it was not uncommon for unwelcome newborns to be strangled or "exposed"; that is, abandoned for someone to rescue or for wild animals and birds to devour. Thus the second-century epistle attributed to Barnabas said, "You shall not kill either the fetus by abortion or the newborn," and the philosopher Athenagoras in 177 urged the Emperor Marcus Aurelius to "call women who take medications to induce an abortion murderers," and to "forbid the exposure of a child, because it is the same as killing a child." A series of such exhortations resulted in the outlawing of infanticide shortly after the Emperor Constantine extended religious tolerance to Christians and Christianity grew to become the privileged religion of state.

To be sure, confusion entered into the church's position, for the church long accepted Aristotelian theory of delayed ensoulment, including a time distinction be-

Facts, Myths and Maybes

tween ensoulment in male and female fetuses; i.e., the fortieth day for a male, eightieth day for a female. In fact, it was not until 1869 that the church formally rejected the distinction between a formed (ensouled) and unformed (unsouled) fetus, and thus ended esoteric discussion—which had affected neither preaching nor practice—over the lawfulness or unlawfulness of aborting an unsouled fetus. The church consistently held that it was an evil act to destroy the life of a fetus. Not acceptable were Aristotelian nuances, nor contentions about the fetus being an unjust aggressor, nor the rights of a woman over her own body. Abortion was a wrong, a violation of Natural Law and of the Fifth Commandment.

This unwavering position of the church carries the weight of popes and of councils, including Vatican II, which said in *Gaudium et spes*, the Constitution on the Church in the Modern World, that ". . . from the moment of conception life must be guarded with greatest care, while abortion and infanticide are unspeakable crimes" (51). As it was at Vatican II, so it was in the beginning of Christianity itself.

* * *

Is it not true that in extenuating circumstances the preference in Catholic theology is for the life of the unborn child over that of the mother?

197

John Deedy

NOT SO . . . This dilemma is the stuff of fiction and of film, as in Henry Morton Robinson's 1950 book-cum-movie, *The Cardinal*. Pope Pius XII scorched the preferential notion in a 1951 address. "Never and in no case has the church taught that the life of the child must be preferred to that of the mother," he exclaimed. "It is erroneous to put the question with this alternative: either the life of the child or that of the mother. No, neither the life of the mother nor that of the child can be subjected to an act of direct suppression."

* * *

But does not the church make a distinction between direct and indirect abortion, condemning the former but approving the latter?

TRUE . . . The church says that direct abortion is always wrong, including therapeutic abortions performed for such reasons as abnormalities, social and familial considerations, psychological health of the mother, and the like. Indirect abortion, by distinction, is permissible. This would be an abortion that occurred indirectly as a consequence of medical treatment or a surgical procedure to save the life of the mother, and as a result of which the death of the fetus occurs as a regretted and unavoidable consequence.

The evil is permitted by the church under the principle known as the "double effect," provided four criteria are met: (1) the evil effect is not wished and every reasonable effort is made to avoid it; (2) the immediate effect is good in itself (i.e., saving of the life of the woman); (3) the evil is not made a means in obtaining the good effect (else the end would be justifying the means, an immorality all its own); (4) the good effect is at least as important as the evil effect which follows.

Of course, accidental abortions, as in the instance of non-induced miscarriages, have always been held morally blameless by the church.

* * *

The church's birth-control review of the 1960s was a clear-cut call from the start.

NO WAY . . . From the moment the issue surfaced in the 1960s with the development of the oral contraceptive—"The Pill," so called—birth control was very much up for grabs in the church. The decision could have gone the other way.

To begin with, the principal developer of the pill—a synthetic progesterone that inhibits ovulation—was a Catholic, Dr. John Rock, and his purpose during research was not to discover a new and easy protection against pregnancy, but to overcome sterility in women visiting a reproductive clinic of his in Brookline, Massachusetts. As a committed Catholic, one who at-

199

tended daily Mass and kept a crucifix above his desk, Rock was thoroughly familiar with Catholic teaching about artificial birth control. The last thing he was aiming at was the bringing down of temple walls. Dr. Rock sincerely believed that with the pill he had happened serendipitously on a solution to a controversy that had long racked the church. As Rock was to argue in his book *The Time Has Come* (Knopf, 1963), his discovery did not contravene Catholic doctrine. The pill, he contended, was the equivalent of a "pill-established safe period," like the safe period of the rhythm method of birth control, with which the church, of course, had no objections, and further that it carried the same moral implications as the rhythm method. No natural process was damaged; no organ was mutilated; the anovulants of his research merely served as "adjuncts to nature." It was an argument that persuaded very many theologians and some bishops.

But Rock didn't exactly start it all. Even before his book hit the market, the birth-control issue was alive and in the open. Other medical scientists—notably Dr. Gregory Pincus and Dr. M.C. Chang of the Worcester Foundation for Experimental Biology in Shrewsbury, Massachusetts—were also working on the pill, and field experiments were being conducted in places as socially and religiously disparate as Puerto Rico and Sweden.

Aware of this activity and its implications for Catholic morality, Pope John XXIII quietly established a commission of six members in March of 1963 to advise on the problems of population, the family and natality. Pope John was to die seven months later, but Paul VI continued the commission, expanding it to fifteen members in May 1964, then to fifty-two by March 1965. Theologians dominated the commission. But on it were fifteen demographers or economists, a dozen doctors, and six representatives of the laity, five of whom were women. It was a representative commission, and would become more so with the addition of legal experts and others, bringing the number of members now to sixty-eight.

Speaking to this commission in 1965, Pope Paul stressed the guardianship of life and love, adding, ''In the present case, the problem posed may be summarized as follows: In what form and according to what norms ought spouses to accomplish in the exercise of their mutual love that service of life to which their vocation calls them?'' The charge, as the question itself, seemed open-ended, and the presumption was that the pope, though hardly bound, would be guided by the commission's recommendation.

Well, we know what happened. The commission voted sixty-four to four that change in the church's position on birth control was not only possible but also advisable. An executive committee of cardinals and bishops came to the same conclusion by a vote of nine to six.

John Deedy

Pope Paul, however, on July 29, 1968, issued *Humanae Vitae*, stressing the "indisputable" authority of the papacy, dismissing the conclusions of the commission as not "definitive," citing the church's "coherent teaching" on the nature of marriage, and saying there would be no change. "Every conjugal act must be open to the transmission of life."

Pope Paul asked in his encyclical that its message be received with "joyful docility." We know of course that it wasn't. Clergy rebelled—in the Archdiocese of Washington alone, twenty-five priests were defrocked by Patrick Cardinal O'Boyle. Laity rebelled too . . . not by walking away from the church, but by appropriating birth control as a matter for the individual conscience. Surveys show that upwards of eighty percent of American Catholic women of childbearing age and their spouses now practice artificial birth control.

Thus the matter stands. That open question of the early and mid-1960s is no longer up for grabs. Officially, the matter is closed, and likely to remain so for the indefinite future. Certainly John Paul II won't resurrect it; he has repeatedly invoked *Humanae Vitae* and endorsed its conclusions. But much of the rest of the church has made its judgment, and it isn't as Paul VI or John Paul II would have it. Birth control is a fact of Catholic life. That's the reality. What a future pope might rule on artificial birth control is anyone's guess, but it's no great guess what historians of tomorrow will conclude. They'll say that no one issue so undermined papal authority in the twentieth century than the handling of this one.

* * *

Official Catholic teaching has consistently judged all homosexual acts as unnatural and gravely sinful.

FACT . . . From Saint Paul, through Saint Augustine, through Saint Thomas Aquinas, through the Congregation for the Doctrine of the Faith's 1975 *Declaration on Sexual Ethics* and its 1986 statement on pastoral care of homosexual persons, the church has held genital expression between persons of the same sex, male or female, to be sinful in and of itself.

The church grants that genetic orientation or physiological presence of homosexuality is not *per se* sinful, and further allows that subjective responsibility for one's homosexuality may be conditioned or diminished by compulsion and related factors that diminish free and full consent of the will. Nonetheless, the acting out of one's homosexuality is condemned—condemned, yes, as unnatural and gravely sinful. As the 1975 *Declaration* declares apropos serious sins of the sexual order, "it in no way follows that one can hold the view that . . . mortal sins are not committed." As for homosexual acts, they are labeled "intrinsically disordered" and "in no case [can they] be approved of."

203

John Deedy

Church teaching about homosexuality has lately come under fire from several Catholic quarters as arbitrary, and as physiologically and psychologically unenlightened. Schools of theological thought have weighed in with a variety of counter opinions, among them: that homosexual acts are morally neutral; that the morality of homosexual acts depends on the quality of the relationship between the persons involved; that homosexual acts are essentially imperfect, and are neither always sinful nor an ideal; that while the heterosexual relationship of marriage is "normative," homogenital acts that depart from the "normative" or ideal are the individual's responsibility before God, particularly in instances of those who conclude after pastoral and other counseling that they are not called to celibacy for the Kingdom.

The official church hears but accepts none of this.

Where does all this leave the person grappling in mind, body and conscience over the issue? In *Catholicism* (Winston, 1980), Father Richard P. McBrien proposes eight Christian values that should be taken into account by Catholics and other Christians regarding the moral question of homosexuality:

1. The goodness of procreation, as an expression of mutual love and for the welfare of the human community at large;

2. The personal dignity of every human being, regardless of his or her sexual orientation, and the exis-

tence of natural and civil rights which flow from that dignity;

3. The need of every person for love, friendship, even intimacy, although not necessarily of a genetically sexual nature;

4. The inviolability of conscience;

5. The responsibility to act on an informed conscience;

6. The existence of many internal and external impediments to full human freedom;

7. The right and responsibility of the church to teach on matters pertaining to morality (in McBrien's terminology, "church" means not only the pope and the bishops, but also other qualified teachers with varying degrees of ministerial authority and scientific competence);

8. The duty of Catholics to take such teaching seriously into account in the process of forming their consciences.

* * *

The church is kinder, gentler, less judgmental towards people who are apparent suicides.

MOST CERTAINLY . . . and so too are medical examiners in determining reason (as distinct from cause) of death. The latter commonly issue death certificates that allow the possibility of the deaths having occurred because of accident or mental instability, and these documents are usually accepted by church officials as proof of mitigating circumstances, which in turn permits Christian burial for the deceased. In fact, the new and revised Code of Canon Law (1983) no longer automatically denies Christian burial to those hitherto classified as suicides. The word "suicides" isn't even in the Code. This is remarkable change from the situation which existed up to a generation ago.

Historically, Christians along with Jews held suicide to be an action with mortal moral consequences, specifically as a violation of the Fifth Commandment delivered to Moses on Mount Sinai: "Thou shalt not kill." Both the Jewish and Christian traditions long equated suicide with murder, the act being considered murder of one's self. Accordingly, those who died at their own hand were denied religious burial rites.

Civil governments and certain businesses often were just as rigorous as religions in their attitudes toward suicide. It was not until 1823 that England abolished an act whereby "one who commits murder upon himself" could be ignominiously buried on the highway with a stake driven through the body. And it was not until 1870 that a suicide's goods and chattels were to be no longer forfeited to the crown. Even today in the United States suicide is grounds for the voiding of life-insurance policies.

Not all societies, however, have regarded suicide as

theological travesty, cultural disgrace or automatic demonstration of mental instability. Some Eskimo civilizations were known to practice socially motivated geriatric suicide, with aged members of a group or family going off to freeze to death so that others could exist within available food supplies. Suicide belonged to an ancient and honored cultural and religious tradition in Japan into modern times, while in Brittany at one time incurable sufferers could become indirect suicides by appealing for what was known as the "holy stone." The family would come together, a religious rite would be performed, then the oldest living relative would drop a heavy stone on the sufferer's head, ending that life.

One can well imagine church—state, too, of course—reprobating such practices as those. On the other hand, Jewish tradition honors the defenders of Masada who, in the year 72, slew themselves rather than fall into Roman hands. And of course Catholic theology has always provided for individuals who committed suicide in order to escape rape and sexual defilement. In the main, however, Jewish and Christian traditions over the ages have regarded suicide as an offense to society and more particularly an abrogation of a power—control of life—that belongs exclusively to God.

Periodically this rationale comes under pressure. In the early 1600s, the English poet and churchman John Donne wrote an apology for the principle of suicide,

John Deedy

arguing that "the scandalous disease of headlong dying" was not necessarily and essentially sinful. During the post-World War II cold war between East and West, theologians—Bishop Francis Simon of Indore, India, among them—argued the licitness of direct suicide in cases where an individual with an important secret would be likely to divulge that secret under torture, causing great harm to a large number of people. (This was after it was revealed that the United States was equipping strategic secret agents, like U-2 pilot Francis Gary Powers, with suicide pills. Powers, we know, declined to use his.) Now, of course, in a more secular or, more pertinently, a super-technological age, when life can be prolonged by science to extreme and often undesirable lengths, there are such issues as suicide, direct and indirect, by suicide machines (e.g., Dr. Jack Kevorkian's apparatus that allows people to administer death-inducing drugs to themselves), the foregoing of medical treatment, and the letter of living wills—not all living wills, of course, but certain types of living wills.

Some of these issues affecting life and death—e.g., life-support systems, living wills—the church approaches with caution and nuance. But on direct, premeditated, conscious, rational suicide, whether by hand or machine, the church is unequivocal. The act is evil. If the church gives a Christian burial to an individual who seems to fall into such a category, it only means that it is leaving final judgment up to God. The basic position of the church remains the same. Suicide is an evil, a sin against God, who is the exclusive arbiter of life and death.

* * *

On issues involving modern medical technology, the church is hopelessly retrograde.

NOT SO . . . Some people may not like the positions the church has taken on certain biomedical issues, but its head is hardly in the sands. Never has been, in fact. The church was one of the very first important institutions, religious or otherwise, to confront modern medical technology head on. It was Pope Pius XII, it will be remembered, who spoke out so dramatically, saying that extraordinary means in the care of the terminally ill was not necessary. That was back on February 24, 1957 in an address to the Italian Society of Anesthesiology. Pius XII was careful to rule out all direct forms of euthanasia or mercy killing, but he did allow that a dying patient may be given drugs to relieve his or her pain, even if the treatment might indirectly result in a shortening of life. It was a startling declaration for its time. The pope said: "If there exists no direct causal link, either through the will of the interested parties or by the nature of things, between induced unconsciousness and the shortening of life . . . and if, on the other hand, the actual administration of drugs brings about two distinct effects, the one the relief of pain, the other, the shortening of life, the action is lawful. . . .''

To be sure, medical science, sophisticated as it was, was not nearly so advanced as now, and therefore many of the contingencies encountered today were not covered in Pius XII's address. Not yet common, for instance, were mechanical life-support systems and respirators, devices that in countless circumstances are blessed savers of life, but devices which can turn into instruments of torture when they prolong the dying process almost endlessly. Yet, however dated the pope's address in terms of today's medical and scientific complexities, it did put the church on the cutting edge.

Whether the church has remained avant-garde is a matter of question. The Congregation for the Doctrine of the Faith's lengthy 1987 document on biomedical technologies, focusing mainly on artificial methods of human reproduction, such as in-vitro fertilization, surrogate motherhood, embryo and sperm banks, was not well received by the scientific community. Aspects of the document also met objections in some Catholic quarters. But at least the document was indication that the church was acutely aware of modern technological issues—it should be; the Pontifical Academy of Sciences has an Advisory Committee for Biotechnology Applied to Man—and that it is determined to have a say in the shaping of these issues. Fair enough.

* * *

The brave new world of biotechnology that has posed so many moral dilemmas for families and for church was opened up by a Catholic monk playing around with peas in a monastery garden.

TRUE . . . and his name was Gregor Mendel. Mendel, an Augustinian father at the Abbey of St. Thomas at Brunn, Austria, opened windows on genetics and the life sciences by elementary experiments in the growing of the common garden-variety pea (*pisum sativum*). This was in mid-nineteenth century.

Mendel experimented in plant hybridization and cross-breeding, focusing especially on the manner by which parental characters were transmitted to progeny, how traits were controlled by pairs of factors, and how traits entered mature sex cells or gametes to form new pairs. His was more avocation than dedicated, life-long scientific research. He indulged his hobby for fifteen years, then abruptly broke it off when elected abbot at age 46 in 1868.

Mendel died in 1884, and on his death the new abbot had his notebooks and scientific records burned as useless. But squirreled away in an obscure scientific journal was a paper that Mendel had published in 1865, and it would have sudden, worldwide impact when reviewed in 1900. Mendel, it developed, had plotted the route to Aldous Huxley's brave new world; he had unlocked the principles of genetics and inheritance—principles science now calls Mendel's Laws. They are: (1) the Law of Segregation (a hybrid or heterozygote transmits to each mature sex cell or gamete only one factor, not two, of the pair received from the parent) and (2) the Law of Independent Assortment (different characters, such as shape and color, are recombined at random in the gametes).

At first Mendel's theories were applied to plants and animals: tomatoes, hens, horses, that sort of thing. But discoveries in those fields led inevitably to the human person and ultimately the spiraling molecule that is the life strand in all living cells: deoxyribonucleic acid or DNA. Amazingly, no fewer than three billion DNA base-pair genes make up the individual or human genome.

Today many moralists worry about science playing God, and it is not an insignificant worry when the very elements of life can be fused in a test tube through *in vitro* fertilization, manipulated so as to determine characteristics such as eye color or left- or right-handedness, or assigned to a third party through surrogate parenthood. With all that, the world opened by Mendel is just being glimpsed. As Huxley once wrote in related context, we understand about as much of the biosciences "as a worm in a flower pot on a balcony in London knows of the life of the great city around him."

Again, the phenomenon of biotechnology traces back to an Augustinian monk. To be sure, the bioscientific and biotechnological world would exist without Gregor Mendel. By 1900 scientists like Hugo de Vries, Carl Correns and Erik von Tschermak were also on the track of hybrid ratios, and though Mendel's paper immediately solved for them the riddle of their research, undoubtedly they or their successors would have independently formulated the answers of Mendel. Still Gregor Mendel, the Augustinian, was there first.

The church hasn't yet got around to celebrating the fact that the father of genetics was one of its own, and an ordained one at that. Mendel, indeed, seems to be regarded as something of a modern-era Galileo, too dangerously innovative for everyone's good. He is passed over in silence. But the day will come.

Incidentally, Gregor Mendel never managed to pass the state examination to qualify as a teacher. He attempted it twice, failed twice, and never tried again. At the Abbey of Saint Thomas, he was for years nothing more than a temporary uncertified teacher. Maybe that's why his papers were eventually burned.

*   *   *

213

John Deedy

The Catholic Church is unqualifiedly opposed to genetic engineering.

WHOA! . . . The church, as noted, has condemned new biomedical technologies in areas of human reproduction, but intervention in normal human reproduction processes is only one aspect of genetic engineering.

First, let's get straight what genetic engineering is. Quoting from Thomas A. Shannon's *What Are They Saying About Genetic Engineering?* (Paulist Press, 1985), genetic engineering "refers to specific technical interventions in the structure of the gene for a variety of purposes, including, but not limited to, removing a deleterious or harmful gene, changing the genetic structure of a particular organism, or enhancing a particular genetic capacity. Genetic engineering is a specific intervention into the actual gene structure itself." In a broader sense, however, and the way the term is commonly understood, "genetic engineering refers to the possibility of not only designing our descendants, but also manipulating the entire ecosystem for a variety of purposes." More specifically, "genetic engineering in a broad sense refers to technologies such as in vitro (or test tube) fertilization, cloning (the artificial reproduction of an identical twin), recombinant DNA research, and a variety of other applications of this knowledge of the gene structure,

214

together with the social, political, and ethical dimensions of these applications.''

That's a mouthful to be sure, but it gives an idea of how vast the science is, and how great the potentials are for mischief and outright evil, but also for good.

Apropos the good, all sorts of possibilities exist, including control of every major genetically caused disease. A simple blood test, for example, can be used to spot a health problem, then corrections made to repair the defective genes or to alter their interplay. Already there are any number of instances of genetic abnormalities being spotted in fetuses, which have been corrected by surgery or gene splicing while the fetus was still in the womb. Science, in fact, is increasingly capable of closing in on everything with a genetic key, from Alzheimer's disease to high blood pressure.

Condemn genetic engineering, therefore, in toto? Impossible. The church cannot, and is too humanitarian to do so. But abuses of genetic engineering? That is another matter entirely. The church has no recourse but to speak out. For instance, church moralists question fetal-cell implant surgery in the treatment of Parkinson's disease. The implants show great promise in fighting the muscular rigidities and tremors of the disease, but where does the fetal tissue for these implants come from? It is obtained primarily from elective abortions. Instance: the story in the news not long ago of the young woman purposefully becoming pregnant and undergoing an abortion in order to produce fetal tissue for her grandfather's treatment of Parkinson's. On cases like that the church does indeed draw the line.

But as said, the field is vast. In 1977, quite early-on actually, the American bishops focused on recombinant DNA research through their Committee for Human Values. They cautioned against a utilitarian or simple risk-benefit approach, and against rushing ahead to accomplish all possible goods of which science suddenly seems capable. The danger, they said, was of science and medicine becoming entrapped in the technological imperative of doing something just because it is possible to do so. There is a need, the bishops said, to evaluate whether future generations will benefit from the pursuit of interesting but possibly unnecessary scientific research. Fair enough, once again.

The problem, alas, is that developments in genetic engineering have proceeded at such a pace that it has been impossible for moralists to keep up. A similar gap exists in the public arena. There just hasn't been time to enter into equations issues of public policy and all the ethical questions involved.

* * *

Facts, Myths and Maybes

The withdrawal of life-support systems from the terminally ill is really a form of euthanasia, or mercy killing.

MYTH . . . Euthanasia, or mercy killing, is the direct causing of death to end a person's suffering from an infirmity, painful disease or difficult condition, such as old age. It is a sin against the Fifth Commandment, "Thou shalt not kill." It is always wrong.

Moralists caution, however, against confusing euthanasia and withdrawal of life-support systems in instances where these systems are no longer in the best interests of the hopelessly sick person, and where a distinction has been drawn by the responsible parties between the use of ordinary means and extraordinary means in the continuation of life in the specific circumstances of the person who is gravely and incurably ill. One refers back to Pius XII in an earlier entry. Extraordinary means are not demanded in the care of hopelessly sick persons, and one may legally and morally switch to low-technology, comfort care, the effect of which may be to allow the inevitable death to occur.

Similarly, and again alluding back to Pius XII, the use of drugs in these cases to relieve suffering may be permitted, even though this use might result in a shortening of life. The use is permitted under the principle of the double effect. (The double effect is the close relation of two results—the one good, the other bad—from a single action. The action is morally justifiable,

217

John Deedy

provided certain criteria are met. Specifically, the action must be good in itself; there must be a proportionality between the good and bad effects; the bad effect must be neither directly intended nor sought.)

A more sticky question, and one the church has not definitely resolved, is the withdrawal of nutrition and hydration to end a procedure that no longer benefits patients, specifically those in a persistent vegetative state (PVS), or to prevent them from becoming entrapped in technology. Several years ago officials of the Diocese of Providence supported the discontinuation of food and water in the case of one Marcia Grey, since there was no "reasonable hope of recovery" and the medical procedures in use were "disproportionate and unduly burdensome." However, a 1988 survey of U.S. diocesan bioethics committees published in the Jesuit journal *Theological Studies* shows splits in several directions on whether feeding tubes constituted ordinary or extraordinary means of treatment, and therefore whether the withholding or the forgoing of such treatment was morally justifiable.

Biomedical ethicists Thomas A. Shannon of Worcester Polytechnic Institute and James J. Walter of Loyola University of Chicago argued in connection with that survey that it was "inappropriate" to characterize the withdrawal of medical nutrition and hydration from PVS patients as euthanasia. The motivation, they said, is not to intend the death of a patient either by commission or omission, for this would constitute euthanasia. Their distinction: "The patient's death, while foreseen, results from the justified discontinuance of a technology that itself can neither correct the underlying fatal pathology, i.e. the permanent inability to ingest food and fluids orally, nor offer the patient any reasonable hope for what we have defined as quality of life"—namely, the relationship which exists between the medical condition of the patient, on the one hand, and the patient's ability to pursue life's goals and purposes, understood as the values that transcend physical life, on the other.

Shannon and Walter stressed that they were not arguing the forgoing or withdrawing of tube-feeding medical technology as a mandatory practice, but rather as a moral option.

In 1992, a committee of the U.S. Conference of Catholic Bishops addressed the question, and warned against the practice of withdrawing food and liquid from irreversibly unconscious patients. However, it called its statement "our first word, not our last word," acknowledging that official Catholic teaching had not reached definite conclusions on all the moral issues surrounding withdrawal of treatment.

* * *

John Deedy

The Catholic Church is opposed to living wills and health care proxy arrangements of whatever sort.

FALSE . . . The church is cautious on this issue, but basically it has no problems with health care proxy arrangements—provided, where there is legitimate freedom of decision, the personal convictions and preferences of the care recipient are respected, and that proxies act in compliance with authentic teaching of the church. The situation in Massachusetts is a case in point demonstrating the church's attitude in this area of human concern.

In 1991 the Massachusetts State Legislature debated and subsequently adopted a so-called "living will bill," which allows individuals, eighteen years of age or older, to choose an agent or proxy to make health decisions for them should they lose the ability to decide for themselves. The Massachusetts Catholic Conference, representing the Archdiocese of Boston and the Dioceses of Worcester, Springfield and Fall River, opposed the bill, but, as it went to pains to point out, its problem was with the legislation itself, *not the concept* of a living will.

In context of the latter, the conference quoted a section of the Vatican's May 5, 1980, Declaration on Euthanasia: "When inevitable death is imminent in spite of the means used, it is permitted in conscience to take the decision to refuse forms of treatment that would only secure a precarious and burdensome prolongation of life, so long as the normal care due to the sick person in similar cases is not interrupted . . . In the final analysis, it pertains to the conscience either of the sick person, or of those qualified to speak in the sick person's name, or of the doctors, to decide, in the light of moral obligations and of the various aspects of the case.''

The Massachusetts Catholic Conference's objection with the proposed bill hinged mainly on details of legality rather than ideology or morality. It regarded living-will legislation under debate as unnecessary, contending that a legal consensus already existed on the subject, and that passage of the bill would only add another layer of law in an area of human decision where moral and legal right already existed to refuse disproportionate (extraordinary) medical care.

As mentioned, the bill passed despite the conference's opposition, and went into effect in the closing weeks of 1991. The Massachusetts Catholic Conference could have begun a campaign for repeal, but adopted a wiser course instead. Through diocesan newspapers, social agencies, church-door distribution and the like, it provided to Catholics across the state an eight-page guide on the health care issue, together with a standard, acceptably Catholic health care proxy form.

John Deedy

One of the guide's most useful features was a presentation of Catholic teaching relevant to personal health care decisions. Its seven points follow:

1. All human life is sacred, from the first moment of conception to the time of natural death.

2. All human beings, regardless of physical or mental abilities, share an equal human dignity meriting both respect and protection.

3. Catholics are free to make health decisions regarding the use of extraordinary means to prolong a life in a terminal illness in accordance with Catholic moral teaching.

4. Suffering is a mystery. The role of medicine is to relieve the suffering of the sick by diligent research and compassionate treatment. Suffering which cannot be alleviated can become redemptive when united with the suffering love of Christ.

5. Human persons are obligated to take reasonable care of their own health by preserving and nurturing it with appropriate and ordinary (proportionate) means. But, the human person is not obligated to use extraordinary (disproportionate) measures to prolong life in this world; that is, measures offering no reasonable hope or measures involving excessive hardship.

6. Respect for unborn human life requires that life-sustaining treatment be extended to a dying pregnant patient if continued treatment can benefit the child.

7. An agent designated as a health care proxy never

can be authorized to deny the basic personal services every patient rightfully can expect; such as bed rest, hygiene, and appropriate pain medication. Nutrition and hydration should always be provided when they are capable of sustaining human life.

Persons seeking further information on the subject of living wills and health care proxies may contact the Massachusetts Catholic Conference at 60 School Street, Boston, MA 02108 (tel. 617-523-4860); or The Catholic Health Association of the United States, 4455 Woodson Road, St. Louis, MO 63134 (tel. 314-427-2500).

*   *   *

Catholics who arrange for the cremation of a loved one, or who ask cremation for themselves in their wills, are in defiance of the letter of church law.

MYTH . . . The new Code of Canon Law (1983) condemns cremation only in the instance of those who choose "cremation of their bodies for reasons opposed to the Catholic faith" (Canon 1184, sections 1 and 2). It is true that the church "earnestly recommends that the pious custom of burial be retained" (Canon 1176, section 3), but contrary to popular mythology, it does not outlaw cremation. In fact, in Canada the ashes of one who is cremated ("cremains," so called) are even permitted in the church for the funeral Mass of the deceased. As of this writing (1992), this is not the case in the U.S., but that's only because the American bishops have not taken the formality of asking Rome's permission on the matter. A move is under way in this regard.

Actually all this represents no great change, for cremation was never at odds with church dogma. The canonical ban some remember was not even in place until 1886. Hitherto cremation was a muted issue. Periodically the church would speak in support of the traditional Christian practice of burial, and there was an occasional excoriation—as in 1300 when Pope Boniface VIII (1294-1303) condemned the boiling of human remains to separate flesh from bones, a grisly practice among Christians who died a distance from their homeland, as while on a Crusade. (The procedure made easier the transportation of remains for burial in one's homeland.) The church did not have to worry about cremation, because the practice never existed in any wide sense. To be sure, cremation was common in ancient times, and some Greek and Roman sects favored the practice in the belief that it sped the dead to the land of shadows. But from early in the Christian era, the norm for disposal of a dead person was burial in the ground.

In fact, in the early Christian era cremation was less a social preference than it was a tool of persecutors.

Facts, Myths and Maybes

Romans were burying their dead. So too were Christians in pious emulation of the crucified Christ. Christians believed that as Christ was resurrected from the dead, so one day would they. For persecutors, then, the cremating of a Christian's body became a way of attacking Christian belief in the body's resurrection in the Lord. The persecutors believed cremation made resurrection forever impossible.

Early church leaders rejected that notion. As the third-century writer Minucius Felix put it: "Nor do we fear, as you suppose, any harm from the [mode of] sepulture, but we adhere to the old, and better, custom [of burial]." The Council of Nicaea (325) affirmed belief in the body's resurrection with words recited to this day in the Creed of the Mass: "We acknowledge one baptism for the forgiveness of sins. We look for the resurrection of the body, and the life of the world to come."

Note there were no qualifiers at Nicaea involving burial or cremation, but then again there was hardly any need. Cremation had become uncommon, and after the fifth century was virtually unheard of in the Christian world, except in times of pestilence and disaster when large numbers of dead overwhelmed authorities and cremation became necessary as a public-health measure.

But cremation made a comeback, and a number of

225

John Deedy

factors were responsible, some of them secularist, some of them biological. The time was early nineteenth century.

In a world awakening to the dangers of germ-carrying microorganisms, physicians and chemists began to raise questions of public hygiene. Might the traditional cemetery be a health hazard? Might it be polluting underground or nearby water supplies? Might a neighborhood's air be fouled if it bordered or surrounded a cemetery? Might soil near a cemetery be poisoned by decomposing remains? Might cremation eliminate all these concerns?

As these questions were being debated, governments in crowding western Europe passed laws recognizing cremation as an acceptable funeral custom, partly as a land-conservation measure. Those moves spawned cremation societies in major cities throughout Europe, and the church suddenly grew wary.

Bacteriological studies dispelled public-hygiene worries about traditional burial, but those cremation societies were a problem. The church viewed them as materialist and anti-Christian, and issued the alluded to decree of 1886 banning membership in such societies, at the same time declaring it unlawful for Catholics to demand cremation for their own body or that of another. Reaffirmations of the policy came from the Holy Office in 1925 and 1926. Proponents of cremation were branded "enemies of Christianity."

226

Facts, Myths and Maybes

Catholic ground seemed firm on the subject, but it shifted in 1963. On the eve of Vatican II, the Holy Office (now the Congregation for the Doctrine of the Faith) declared cremation an acceptable alternative to burial. The faithful were exhorted to continue the practice of inhumation (burial), but goodwill was presumed for those preferring cremation.

As for the growing preference in recent years for cremation, several factors are at work, and very likely some have influenced the church's change of policy. One factor is convenience. Land really isn't unlimited. Many urban cemeteries are full, and sometimes the nearest one with space available is twenty or thirty miles away. Another factor is cost. Cremation can be relatively inexpensive—in the U.S., several hundred dollars versus $3000 to $4000, on the average, for a traditional burial. Psychological considerations also seem to be a factor; the very thought of burial can trigger claustrophobic reactions in many people.

In any instance, the number of cremations is increasing—by 7 to 8 percent a year in the U.S. It is estimated that by the year 2000, 25 percent of all deaths in the U.S. will be followed by cremation; it is presently at 16.1 percent. Catholics are part of that trend, albeit at a rate estimated at half that of the general society. But cremation is growing in the Catholic community—and to no one's particular consternation.

IV

Culture & Tradition

Culture and tradition, in the context of this book, may be said to be the hand-me-downs of faith and belief. However pious and inspirational, they do not involve dogma or formal belief. They are not essential. There are serious, important elements in culture and tradition. But so much also is artifact of two millennia of existence, of life and worship in the church, handed down generation to generation, until they have become, as Benedictine Father J.B. McLaughlin wrote years ago, part of "a running stream of witness" to the church's belief—indeed, its very survival. Some aspects of culture and tradition are silly; some border on absolute inanity. Still they comprise part of the whole, and thus belong to that sum of qualities that make the church what it is.

John Deedy

The relaxing of eucharistic fast regulations was an innovation of Vatican Council II.

MYTH . . . The change in Eucharistic fast regulations was rather an innovation born of World War II. For centuries the church required Catholics in good health to fast from midnight in order to receive communion on any given day. The fast included water, along with all foods and other liquids, and there were no exceptions, not even for small sips of water taken while half-asleep in the middle of the night. Any intake of whatever kind broke the fast, and one could not receive that day.

The regulation was changed by Pope Pius XII (1938-1958) to accommodate the requests of military chaplains so that they could celebrate Mass at any hour for the welfare of the troops. But the privilege was strictly a military one. Change for the faithful generally did not come until Pius XII approved evening Mass on holydays of obligation (that was in 1953), and later when he extended the holyday evening Mass exception to First Fridays and occasions of religious solemnity (1957.

For ordinary people in the pews, change came in two steps.

First, there was the apostolic constitution of January 16, 1953, *Christus dominus,* declaring that water did not break the eucharistic fast—though one still had to fast from food and other liquids from midnight in order to receive communion. Exceptions were provided for travellers and those engaged in energy-sapping work; they could take liquids (alcohol excepted) up to one hour before Mass and communion.

Those relaxations and the increasing popularity of evening Masses led logically to *Sacram communionem*, Pius XII's *motu proprio* of March 19, 1957, which reduced the eucharistic fast to three hours from solid food and one hour from liquids, alcohol again excepted; a three-hour fast was required from alcohol.

Pius' successor once removed, Pope Paul VI (1963-1978), in turn reduced the eucharistic-fast time frame to one hour from solid food and liquids (alcohol three hours). That was in 1964. The regulation is in place today.

* * *

Then, the fish-on-Friday change was an innovation of Vatican II.

WRONG AGAIN . . . The abrogation of the Friday-abstinence law was probably made in the spirit of the Council, but it had nothing to do with Vatican II per se. The initiative was Paul VI's, and was enunciated in the apostolic constitution of February 17, 1966, *Poenitemini.*

Poenitemini provided changes in a number of dietary

John Deedy

disciplines, but the news bombshell was that Catholics could now eat meat on Friday. This was startling change, as generations of Catholics had been brought up to believe that eating meat on Friday wasn't just a sin, it was a mortal sin. This was no ordinary discipline. One could burn in hell for all eternity for enjoying that filet mignon on Friday.

Catholic source books were emphatic on the point; e.g., the 1913 *Catholic Encyclopedia:* ". . . the law of abstinence [on Friday] embodies a serious obligation whose transgression, objectively considered, ordinarily involves a mortal sin. The unanimous verdict of theologians, the constant practice of the faithful, and the mind of the church place this point beyond cavil."

However, though now one was no longer going to go to hell for eating meat on Friday, one was expected to respect the day as one of penitence, the basic requirements of which consisted, in Pope Paul's words, of "prayer—fasting—charity," with peoples of the world's richer nations expected to practice self-denial and charity on behalf of "their brothers who suffer in poverty and in hunger, beyond all boundaries of nation and continent." It was left to individual bishops' conferences to decide exactly what those practices should be. The U.S. bishops encourage works of penance, but it is safe to say that for most American Catholics the ordinary Friday is now no different than any other day of the week.

232

Facts, Myths and Maybes

Interestingly enough, in 1984 the French bishops reinstated the practice of Friday abstinence, but extended the abstinence options from meat so as to include tobacco or alcohol.

* * *

The Ember Days of fast and abstinence are gone the way of Friday abstinence.

EVEN MORE SO . . . Ember Days are gone completely, eliminated by article 331 of the "Instruction on Particular Calendars" issued by the Congregation for the Sacraments and Divine Liturgy on June 24, 1970.

For those who have forgotten or indeed never heard of Ember Days, they were penitential days of fast and abstinence arranged in four triads around the four seasons of the year. They were observed on Wednesdays, Fridays and Saturdays in the weeks following the first Sunday of Lent, Pentecost (seventh Sunday after Easter), September 14 (Feast of the Exaltation of the Cross), and December 13 (Feast of Saint Lucy). On Ember Days Catholics not only were required to fast, but also to abstain from meat. The purpose of Ember Days was the sanctification of the seasons, with Ember Saturdays marked especially for God's blessing on priests.

The origin of Ember Days is obscure, though they can be traced back to the third century. They were prescribed for observance in the universal church by Pope Gregory VII (1073-1085).

Ember Days were formally in place then a full nine centuries before the 1970 Instruction to dioceses to substitute in their stead "days or periods of prayer for the fruits of the earth, prayer for human rights and equality, prayer for world justice and peace, and penitential observance outside Lent."

Replaced at the same time were Rogation Days. Known since the fifth century, Rogation Days were of lesser solemnity than Ember Days; there was no fasting or abstinence, for instance. In the main they were times of special prayer for a bountiful harvest, for protection against calamity, and for penance for sins. Their elimination is likewise covered by the days of prayer called for in the 1970 Instruction.

With the suppression of Ember Days, Lent remains the last of the church's old-time penitential seasons.

* * *

The observance of Lent dates back to the Apostles.

MYTH . . . In the fifth century, some Fathers claimed that Lent was of apostolic institution, but the claim is doubtful. From earliest Christian times everyone agreed that a penitential season should precede the solemnities of Easter, but for at least three centuries there was no agreement over how long that should be. Saint Irenaeus, writing around the year 190, clued to the diversity of opinion, saying: "some think they ought to fast for one day, others for two days, and others even for several, while others reckon forty hours both of day and night to their fast." Apparently he knew nothing about any Lent or pre-Easter fast of forty days, else he would have mentioned it.

In the fourth century Saint Athanasius enjoined the people of Alexandria to observe a forty day period of fasting prior to Easter, indicating that this was the mode now practiced throughout Christendom. ". . . [W]hile all the world is fasting, we who are in Egypt should not become a laughing stock as the only people who do not fast but take our pleasure in those days," Athanasius wrote. The year was 339, and Athanasius was recently back from a trip to Europe, including Rome.

Some sources allege that the forty-day Lent was not known in the West until the time of Saint Ambrose (c339-397). The date of Athanasius' letter would seem to negate that theory.

So, no, our Lent does not date from the time of the Apostles. But apparently it was observed before the year 339. That's early enough.

* * *

John Deedy

Lent was fixed at forty days in commemoration of the forty hours that Christ laid in the tomb between his death and resurrection.

MYTH . . . As no one knows the exact number of hours that Christ was entombed, so no one knows precisely why forty days was designated the length of Lent. Likely as not, the number can be traced less to some mystical or theological reason than to chance or circumstance, such as the special significance numbers had on the psyches of early peoples.

The rhetorical and symbolic use of numbers was prevalent throughout early societies, and indeed is a notable feature of biblical literature itself. The number one, for example, is basic to the doctrine of monotheism (one God); three, to the idea of completeness (of beginning, middle and end; Father, Son and Holy Spirit); ten, to the idea of wholeness and deduction (the ten fingers of the hand being counting digits and thus the basis of the decimal system).

The significance of the number four derived of the four cardinal directions (north, south, east, west), and forty acquired a sacredness as a multiple of four, being used to indicate a fairly long (though not indefinite) period of time in terms of human existence.

The figure forty was used both in terms of years and days. There were, for example, the forty-year reigns of David and Solomon, and by contrast the forty-days' flood that Noah survived in the ark. In the New Testament there were the forty days and forty nights that Christ fasted in the dessert (Matthew 4:2; Mark 1:13; Luke 4:2), and the forty days that Christ remained on earth after his resurrection (Acts 1:3).

The number forty also had import in terms of human endurance. Paul, for instance, wrote of receiving "forty lashes less one" while held a prisoner (2 Corinthians 11:24).

So how come forty days for Lent? Your guess is as good as anyone's.

*   *   *

The first day of Lent, Ash Wednesday, was sometimes known as Memento Day.

FACT . . . The variant title came from the first word in the Latin injunction spoken by the priest as ashes were signed on the foreheads of the faithful: *Memento, homo, quia pulvis es, et in pulverem reverteris,* "Remember, man, that thou art dust, and unto dust thou shalt return." The formula comes from Genesis 3:19.

That Latin form for the distribution of ashes takes one back some years, of course. Under the new liturgy, the injunction is spoken in the vernacular. Also, the distributor of ashes may be a lay person, male or female, not just a priest. The ashes are acquired from the burning of palms left over from Palm Sunday of the previous year.

Two other points:

1. In the new consciousness over sexist language, most of those distributing ashes drop the ''man'' reference from the signing.

2. An alternate injunction may now be used in preference to the traditional one; namely, ''Turn away from sin and be faithful to the Gospel'' (Mark 1:15).

The Ash Wednesday/Memento Day ritual traces from the fourth century, and is a devotional adaptation of a practice connected with the temporary excommunication and reconciliation of public sinners. By the eleventh century, the ritual was common in all churches for all the faithful, being intended as a reminder of one's mortality and of the need to repent and do penance during the lenten season.

*   *   *

The lenten fast that begins on Ash Wednesday ends at noon on Holy Saturday.

FALSE . . . According to number 28 of the General Norms for the Liturgical Year and the Calendar, Lent extends ''from Ash Wednesday until the Mass of the Lord's Supper exclusive''—that is, until Holy Thursday evening. Technically, therefore, the lenten fast, which is penitential, ends at that time.

Fasting, however, does continue on Good Friday (mandated by church law) and on Holy Saturday (recommended rather than mandated). This, though, is known as the paschal fast, an anticipatory fast preparatory to celebration of the Easter feast.

At one time major feast days of the church, including holydays such as the Assumption and All Saints' Day, were preceded by a day of fast and of abstinence from meat. Those fasts were eliminated in the reforms spoken on in a preceding entry. The paschal fast is thus, strictly speaking, a remnant of the old rule requiring fasting on the vigils of important ecclesiastical feasts.

* * *

The weekdays of Holy Week were once holydays of obligation.

FACT . . . In the proliferation of feast days during the Middle Ages, the weekdays of Holy Week were indeed included as holydays of obligation. In fact, there were so many holydays on the calendar that there were eighty-five days of the year when no servile work could be done and ninety-five days when no court sessions could be held. It was a problem just to get the routine work of church and the society done. Pope Urban VIII

John Deedy

(1623-1644) simplified the arrangement in 1642. Among the holydays eliminated were those of Holy Week.

* * *

The Index of Forbidden Books (Index Librorum Prohibitorum) *is effectively dead and buried.*

TRUE . . . The Index of Forbidden Books passed from meaningfulness on June 14, 1966, when Paul VI (1963-1978), through the Congregation of the Doctrine of the Faith, declared that the Index and its penalties of excommunication no longer had the force of church law. The Congregation still "reviews" books, as we know from recent case histories of Fathers Hans Küng, Edward Schillebeeckx and former priest Leonardo Boff, so therefore a censorship is still at work. Authors can be and indeed are disciplined if their works run afoul of Rome and the authors refuse to revise them. However, unlike the old days, there's no Index to which the books can be consigned and held as condemned.

Paradoxically, few people ever saw a copy of the Index, and fewer still could name books that were on it. Nonetheless, the Index was an enormous embarrassment. For the world at large it stood as the great symbol of Catholic authoritarianism and mind control. The onus was around for centuries.

The Index made its appearance in 1559 during the reign of Paul IV (1555-1559), and received its "modern" codification in 1753 under Benedict XIV (1740-1758). Occasionally the Index would be pruned, but by 1900 it still ran some 450 pages. A 1930 edition needed 563 pages to cover the more than 7,000 titles. A precise count of the number of books on the Index was never possible as some entries would cite the author's name with the notation *opera omnes* ("all works") or *omnes fabulae amatoriae* ("all love stories").

Many of the books on the Index were obscure works of theology or philosophy, but there were also works by some of history's most famous writers and thinkers —people such as Addison, Goldsmith, Victor Hugo, Spinoza, Bergson, Bacon, Bossuet, Kant, Descartes, Heine, Hobbes, Locke, Sir Thomas Browne, Lord Acton, Milton and Balzac. The indiscriminate nature of the Index made it even more of a laughing stock.

A further embarrassment was that the Index targeted some of the church's most orthodox thinkers. Robert Bellarmine, who one day would be canonized as a Doctor of the Church, nearly landed on the Index for contending in *De controversis* that in temporal matters the authority of the pope was not immediate and direct, but flowed indirectly from his spiritual authority. Sixtus V (1585-1590) was furious over the suggestion, but died before he could enforce a decision to put *De controversis* on the Index. His successor, Urban VII (1590) reigned only twelve days before dying of malaria, but he managed to kill Sixtus' proposal.

Similarly, Thomas a Kempis' *Imitation of Christ* once landed on the Index, and there were even red faces in Rome. Apologists explained that it was only the Sebastiano Castellione edition that was banned.

* * *

If the Index is dead, then so too are the old Nihil Obstat *and* Imprimatur *requirements of Catholic publishing.*

WRONG . . . Pre-publication clearance is still necessary for catechisms and other works of religious formation, including editions of Sacred Scripture and books dealing with questions of theology, canon law and church history, and with religious or moral disciplines. In order to be used as texts in educational and instructional settings, works in these fields must be approved by "competent ecclesiastical authority." That is, these works must carry the imprint *Nihil Obstat* ("Nothing stands in the way") of an authorized ecclesiastical censor, and the *Imprimatur* ("Let it be printed") of the bishop where the writer lives or where the work is published. The specifics are spelled out in the new Code of Canon Law, Canons 822-832.

Though these articles of Canon Law are not binding on works not to be used as "textbooks for teaching," the code nonetheless recommends pre-publication clearance as the prudent course. The recommendation is in place though neither the *Nihil Obstat* nor the

242

Facts, Myths and Maybes

Imprimatur is guarantee of the orthodoxy of the work, its viewpoint or its treatment of the subject matter.

Canons 822-832 notwithstanding, the reality is that very few writers or publishers bother these days about securing a *Nihil Obstat* or *Imprimatur*. Indeed, it isn't even easy finding how to go about getting those ecclesiastical *Good Housekeeping* stamps of approval. Most diocesan directories don't list its censors anymore. It's as if the censoring function were dead. By way of example, recent inquiries in an Eastern diocese about how to go about getting a *Nihil Obstat* and *Imprimatur* drew blanks from several officials, before someone suggested trying the office of Vicar for Canonical Affairs.

* * *

Traditionally, the church regarded miracles as being reserved to it as proof of God's favor and as continuing confirmation of the truth of Catholic Christian revelation.

TRUE . . . As Christ worked miracles as external proofs of divine revelation—in other words, as proofs that the God of truth approved his teaching—so indeed has the church believed that the power of miracles belongs only to it, and generally for the very reasons stated in the proposition. Vatican Council I (1869-1870) anathematized those who said "that by miracles the divine order of the [Catholic] Christian religion is not rightly proved," while Vatican Council II (1962-1965) less

243

apocalyptically said that miracles confirmed ''the kingdom has already arrived on earth'' (Dogmatic Constitution on the Church, 5). Supported by teachings such as these, the *New Catholic Encyclopedia* (1967) cautiously maintained that the only true miracles were so-called Catholic miracles.

The problem is, how can miracles be reserved to the Catholic Church and how can miracles ''rightly prove'' implied exclusive favor with God, when as Vatican II taught, God also works through other churches? This being so, might not God then see fit to work miracles through other churches besides the Catholic Church, and do so without at the same time diminishing the Catholic Church's claims on priority of favor? Might not priority of favor actually be a wide or comprehensive manifestation?

Logical questions. Yet the answers may be academic, for miracles seem harder to come by these days. Science is offering explanations for phenomena which were once thought to be without explanation except for divine intervention of a specific kind, so much so that even in the Catholic Church once-upon-a-time requisite numbers of miracles in canonization causes are being waived.

In fact, nowadays it seems that when theologians speak of miracles, the emphasis is less on some dramatic happening than on what occurs interiorly in a person in a particular circumstance—in other words, what happens to that person's mind, body and spirit. If the circumstances of an event work to bring that person closer to God, it is thought by many that may be the true meaning of miracle.

As religion commentator Kenneth Briggs has observed, Pope John Paul II suggested something of this very thing during a 1983 visit to Lourdes. "I have no power to cure you," the pope told pilgrims like himself at the shrine. "Go to the grotto and pray. I can only pray to Christ for you." Then addressing the infirm, he asked that they accept their crosses as a "special mission" and as "interior liberation" that enabled them to lose themselves in divine love "for the sake of humanity."

*　*　*

With the discrediting of Marxism in Eastern Europe, liberation theology is dead in Latin America.

DOUBTFUL . . . except maybe among those who never liked liberation theology from the start. But, first, what are we talking about here?

Liberation theology is a philosophical system originating in Latin America, that would create a more humane society through the refashioning of the social, economic and political structures seen as fostering social injustices. Its essential concern is on behalf of the poor (if liberation theology can be said to have a

John Deedy

catchphrase, it is "the preferential option for the poor"). Thus liberation theology particularly targets for reform those institutions and practices which keep the poor suppressed in the name of economic gain, and economical and political law and order. As presently exercised, for instance, international capitalism would be regarded as a form of economic imperialism.

Liberation theology makes many people nervous, particularly in Rome. For one thing, it is comfortable with Marxist economic theory. Also, the base-level populist communities, *communidades de base,* the backbone of the movement really, are often viewed in the aggregate as a counterpart of the cell system of communism. There is further worry that liberation theology is more sectarian than religious, and that it overidentifies the church with one class of society.

But liberation theology is not Marxism; much less is it incipient communism or so totally secular. In *communidades de base,* for example, local priests provide guidance to community leaders, and in many places the principal focus of the groups is in relating the lessons of the Bible to the day-to-day activities of the members, be they urban slum dwellers or rural *campesinos.* Also, if liberation theology overidentifies the church with the poor, who's to say that this is not a Gospel correction long overdue?

Liberation theology has introduced into Latin-American society (and society elsewhere where it is to be found) a starting point for theological reflection that enables people to test theories against effects. Its particular charism, realized notably through its Christian-based communities, is the ability to make decisions for itself.

Rome has watched liberation theology carefully since its origins in 1968 at the second Latin American Bishop's Conference in Medeillin, Columbia, and has often disciplined or restricted outspoken proponents of the theology, such as Bishop Petro Casaldaliga and former Franciscan theologian Leonardo Boff, both of Brazil. In the process, Rome has issued two "instructions" warning against turning sociology into theology and endorsing violence in social activism, specifically "On Certain Aspects of the Theology of Liberation" (September 3, 1984) and "On Christian Freedom and Liberation" (April 5, 1986).

But an ambivalence is also in place. Rome has not condemned liberation theology outright, but in fact has frequently extended to it a conciliatory velvet glove. More to the point, liberation theology's essential concern for the poor has been newly incorporated into the vision of Rome, sometimes almost word for word out of pro-liberationist documents. Pope John Paul II's 1988 encyclical *Sollicitudo rei socialis*, for example, dwells on "the option or love of preference for the poor . . . to which the whole tradition of the church bears witness," a direct echo of Medellin, 1968, and of Puebla, 1979,

John Deedy

where the Latin American bishops again committed themselves to fight for social change and preferential treatment for the poor.

It is easy to be put off by liberation-theology literature, for it does brim with Marxist phrases and buzz words like praxis, domination, oppressive social structures, etc. But it is a long leap from stereotype to reality, and reality is why liberation theology in Latin America will outlast the judgment that has been rendered against Marxist Communism in Eastern Europe. The loftiness of the liberationist dream enhances theological principle, however vaguely the one, and vague the other might be. Marxism, in sum, would ennoble the worker; it didn't. Liberation theology would ennoble the poor; it does. And it is why it will continue as a force for good.

* * *

Vernacular innovations notwithstanding, Latin is still the official language of the church.

FACT, sort of . . . From the third through nineteenth centuries, Latin was the church's language of currency. Church texts, papal documents and curial decrees invariably were in Latin, and so too were the prayers and lessons of the liturgy—"the better to point out and watch over, in the very bosom of the church, the unity of belief in all places and throughout all times which

248

is her birthright,'' as the old *Catholic Encyclopedia* told us.

The paradox is that for all the reverence accorded the language, Latin was an acquired taste. The original language of Christianity was Aramaic, the Lord's language and the language no doubt of the first Mass. Then for three centuries, Greek was the language of the liturgy. Latin was adopted by the church, because in the Roman ascendancy Latin was the language of commerce, law, literature, politics and the army; it was the language everyone knew; it was the vernacular of the early centuries of the Christian era, and thus before dying as a common means of verbal and written communication, it was the vernacular of the church itself.

The first ecclesial challenges to Latin's dominance came with the spread of the faith to lands beyond the language's reach. Outside Roman orbits, Latin prayers and liturgical texts were so much gibberish. Inevitably, there was pressure for language one could understand, and the result was the introduction of the vernacular into worship and devotional exercises in place after place, the vernaculars in turn becoming the cornerstones of distinctive rites within the Catholic Church.

The Western church in orbit about Rome, home of the Roman or Latin Rite, for centuries resisted trends toward the vernacular—so energetically and effectively, in fact, that there was no such thing even as an English Bible before the Reformation. The Reformation gave great impetus to the vernacular, including in England, whose English tongue was the last of the important European languages without a vernacular Bible. King Henry VIII corrected that, commissioning an English bible in 1530 and having one in hand by 1539. Naturally Rome did not approve of the Great Bible of 1539, as Henry's work was called. Not only was it not in Latin; it was unauthorized and it was "Protestant." Rome would not meet the competition of an English "Protestant" Bible for many decades. It was not until 1582 before there was an authorized Catholic New Testament in English, and it was 1609 before there was a Catholic Old Testament in English.

With the Bible in the vernacular everywhere, the camel's nose was under the tent, so to speak. But Rome hung tough. It continued to transact its affairs in Latin, issue all its decrees in Latin, and insist on Latin in the educating of priests. And it continued to do so for centuries more. But erosion was steady, including in seminaries. Rome fussed, and acted to plug dykes. Just a few months before the opening of Vatican II, for instance, an apostolic constitution appeared over Pope John XXIII's name celebrating Latin for its "immutable" qualities as a language spared the liabilities of modern tongues, where words constantly took on new shades of meaning. *Veterum Sapientia* was quaint, a nostalgic act, the last such indulgence of Pope John's pontificate. It changed nothing; the handwriting was on the wall.

Latin was the language of Vatican Council II, to be sure. The Council, however, was to bury Latin as the universal language of the church.

The process began innocently, with prelates like Boston's Richard Cardinal Cushing complaining of being shut out from the Council's business due to a language barrier. It's "all Greek to me," Cushing remarked mockingly of the Latin proceedings. When asked why he had not intervened on a particular subject, he retorted that linguistically he represented "the Church of Silence." He was not alone in feeling silenced by Latin. Cushing campaigned for simultaneous translation of the Latin presentations into the various vernaculars, offering to pay for the installation of the system himself, if necessary. He won. The system was installed in time for the Council's 1963 session.

Obviously, if Council Fathers needed the vernacular for their deliberations, and indeed profited from it, would not the vernacular also benefit Catholics in the pew in their worship? But of course. Thus the Fathers provided for widespread use of the vernacular in *Sacrosanctum Concilium,* the Constitution on the Sacred Liturgy. Mother tongues were now acceptable for Mass, in the administration of the sacraments, for prayers, chants, readings, directives and most everything else. Bye, bye, Latin.

251

John Deedy

But not completely. Theoretically, Latin remains the church's first language, and just recently the Vatican published a new and expanded Latin dictionary, first in nearly thirty years. At the same time, the only official translations of papal teachings are those in Latin.

Still the grip loosens. Pope John Paul II complained at the 1990 Synod of Bishops that no one was speaking Latin, but as *Newsweek* noted, this lover of the classical language writes his teachings in Polish. As for that new Latin dictionary, *Newsweek* likened it to "the fig leaves on the Vatican's classical statues—a way of hiding the fact that the precise and lovely language of Augustine and Aquinas is no longer accepted or appreciated as the lingua franca of the Roman Catholic Church."

* * *

Once a cardinal, always a cardinal; elevation to the office is neither revocable nor resignable.

MYTH . . . The cardinalate can be withdrawn, it can also be resigned—although instances of either happening are extremely rare.

Cesare Borgia (c1475-1507), one of Pope Alexander VI's seven natural children, and oldest of the four borne by Vannozza Cantanei, his favorite mistress, resigned the red hat. A bishop at 16, an archbishop at 17 and a cardinal at 18, Cesare Borgia quit the cardinalate in 1498 for a dynastic marriage and life as a secular prince. No objections from Alexander VI; Cesare was to take on roles promoting his father's political policies.

On the other hand, the French theologian Louis Billot (1846-1931) lost his red hat. The cause was Billot's sympathies with Action Francaise, the right-wing, anti-republic movement that between the two World Wars stood for the restoration of the French monarchy. Billot had been made a cardinal in 1911 by Pius X, and was the one to place the tiara on Pius XI's head in 1922. After he opposed Pius XI's condemnation of Action Francaise in 1927, he was *persona non grata* with Rome, and was "persuaded" to renounce the cardinalate. Billot retreated to a Jesuit novitiate, there to live out his days.

Modern times have seen one instance more where a churchman's possession of a red hat was threatened.

In 1920, Boston's Cardinal William Henry O'Connell was summoned to Rome by Benedict XV and confronted with evidence that his nephew, who served as archdiocesan chancellor, Monsignor James P.E. O'Connell, was secretly married. Either O'Connell was unaware of the marriage, in which case he was derelict as an administrator, or he was tolerant of the situation, in which case he was a conspirator in a sacrilege. An infuriated Benedict is quoted as telling O'Connell that "the power which gave the red hat could also remove it.'' He never did, presumably in order to contain the scandal surrounding the nephew's case.

* * *

Once a monsignor, always a monsignor.

MYTH, ALSO . . . As an honorary prelate belonging to the pontifical household, a monsignor is easily removed. Certainly, he is subject to the fortunes of whim and circumstance, far more, say, than a cardinal. Pope Benedict XV, for instance, angrily struck Cardinal O'Connell's nephew's name from the list of monsignori at the meeting during which he confronted O'Connell on the nephew's secret marriage.

A monsignor serves, in sum, at the disposition of the pope. So also, ultimately, does a cardinal. The difference is that a monsignor's honorific is renewed from one pontificate to the next, which is not the case with that of a cardinal. Whereas for most monsignori the renewal is pro forma, it isn't always the case. The priest-editor of a Midwest diocesan newspaper, who was a monsignor, lost his rank in the transition from the pontificate of John XIII to that of Paul VI; the priest-editor had incurred the antipathy of the then Apostolic Delegate for printing an article identifying him with a censorship incident at the Catholic University of America.

In any instance, the monsignori honorific is far less

common now than it was in the pre-Vatican II church, having gone the way of many other trappings of triumphalism. There are still monsignori around, but except for the occasional diocese, they're no longer around in epidemic numbers.

* * *

To carry the stigmata—i.e., the wounds or scars of the crucified Christ—is a sure sign of blessedness or sainthood.

MYTH . . . There have been some 341 cases of stigmatization since Saint Francis of Assisi, the first and most celebrated example of the type, but only sixty-two of the individuals have been canonized. The church has always regarded stigmatization as a phenomenon, sometimes even a miraculous one. However, stigmatization does not count as an incontestable miracle, and it is still no substitute for the yardsticks by which sanctity and heroic virtue are usually measured. In a word, the church is cautious. There is always the possibility that the phenomena can be counterfeited or be produced by auto-suggestion or psychotic condition. There may even be natural explanations for certain of the displays; for instance, with the alteration of tissues, exudations of sweat can take on a red cast that could be mistaken for bleeding or a bloody sweat.

Skeptics would also like to know why, if the stigmata are authentic reproductions of the wounds of Christ, those showing the wounds associated with the bar of the cross have them on the hand, not the wrist. Studies show that if Christ were nailed to the cross through the hands, as depicted on most crucifixes, the torso would quickly have toppled over, as the fibers of the hands would not be strong enough to support the body's weight. The nails would have to have been driven through the wrists.

* * *

Since Christ was a man, it follows, as in the "natural resemblance" theory involving ordination, that most stigmatics have been men.

MYTH . . . More than 90 percent of stigmatics have been women, among them Saint Catherine of Siena, who, we are told, first had visible stigmata, but out of humility asked that the wounds be made invisible, and her prayer was answered. The same thing happened with Dominica de Paradis. The church calls that "invisible stigmata."

The better known stigmatics of modern times have been Catherine Emmerich of Muenster (1774-1824), Mary von Moerl of Kaltern, The Tyrol (1812-1868), Louise Lateau of Bois de Haine (1850-1883), Gemma Galgani of Lucca, Italy (1878-1903), now sainted, and Theresa Neumann of Konnersreuth, Germany (1898-1962). The devout will recall that Louise Lateau and Theresa Neumann were also said to have lived exclusively on the Eucharist.

The star of the modern circuit, though, was Francesco Forgione, the Capuchin friar more popularly known as Padre Pio. Padre Pio (1887-1968) bore the stigmata for fifty years, but that was only one of the wonders connected to the man. He was also said to be able to read hearts, which made him a much sought after confessor, and to have had the gift of bilocation; he could be in two places at once. The story is told that without leaving his friary in San Giovanni Rotondo in southern Italy, Padre Pio would appear in distant Rome to console the afflicted or to hear a confession.

In 1947, a young Polish priest visited Padre Pio, and Padre Pio is said to have prophesied, "Someday you will be pope." That priest was Karol Wojtyla, who in 1978 became Pope John Paul II. A worldwide cult exists to Padre Pio.

On the basis of a number of investigations, stigmatics are said to display several common characteristics. Most belong to religious houses; their marks are first displayed during Lent, often on Good Friday; reoccurrence of symptoms, such as bleeding, usually comes on Fridays. One last thing, the wounds of stigmatics are said not to suppurate. They do not grow infected, nor, except for Saint Rita of Cassia, do they give off a fetid odor. In fact, if odor there is, it is said to be rather of lilacs or perfume, as in the instance of Juana of the

Cross of Toledo, Spain, and Blessed Lucy of Narni. Whew!

*   *   *

The church takes the hit as the ogre, the heavy of the Dark Ages.

FACT . . . The question is: How fair all the blame?

The Dark Ages extended roughly from the collapse of the old Roman Empire at the end of the fourth century to the turn of the millennium, the year 1000, and is associated with ignorance and obscurantism. The Catholic Church, having moved into the vacuum created by the Roman Empire's collapse, and suddenly the world's dominant religious and cultural force, is inevitably an obvious target for history's blame-setters.

In a sense the church does bear a measure of blame for the intellectual and cultural darkness that fell over civilization. Given the enormity of the political events connected with the collapse of the Roman Empire, problems would have existed anyway. Still there is little doubt that these problems were exacerbated by the church—specifically through the advancing of Christian philosophy as the culmination of knowledge. With learning, indeed all human activity subsidiary to that which theoretically insured personal salvation, of what importance were other intellectual inquiries and new scholarships? Projected as the individual's highest state of attainment were mystical contemplation and humility, not generalized knowledge and, most especially, not knowledge for knowledge's sake. With such a mindset as this, civilization was obviously on a slippery slope.

Yet the Dark Ages were not the total loss some historians make them, and for this the church can claim credit. Intellectuals such as Boethius, Alcuin, Chordegang of Metz, Cassiodorus, Isidore, Bede, and Clement and Dougal from Ireland kept flames of learning and scholarship flickering. Also, while many rulers were melting down gold, bronze and silver masterpieces for money, and while the populace was breaking up marble sculptures for mortar and recycling marble facades from historic buildings for new construction (often with the church's blessing), religious communities, particularly in Ireland and England, were quietly inaugurating programs of conservation to preserve the heritage others were destroying.

Interestingly enough, the narrow emphasis of the times on mysticism and humility of mind helped spawn the monastic movement, and monasticism in turn produced abbeys that became important centers of learning and depositories of the arts. Monasteries likewise evolved into centers of education, through the establishment of schools originally intended for the training of novices, but eventually broadened to include those not planning religious careers. The Benedictines

259

were notable leaders in this regard. These centers were to prove forerunners of the modern grammar school. The monasteries alone didn't restore light to the ages, but they certainly helped.

No single event or detail of history dispelled the darkness that extended over the six centuries of the Dark Ages. A number of factors came together, two of which merit special mentioning.

First, there was the fact that the world didn't come to an end at the millennium, as many thought it would on the basis of Revelation 20 and its description of dire events to occur on the loosing of Satan after one thousand years of the reign of Christ. The millennium behind them, people could relax and minds could turn to less cosmic matters.

Second, there was the scholastic revival. Today scholasticism is a word of opprobrium, but it was perfect for the new millennium. The writings of Aristotle, Cicero and Seneca were rediscovered, and through scholasticism and the subtleties of Greek and Latin thought development of the mind again assumed importance. There was renewed emphasis on method, on systematic thought, on logic, framed by an awareness of classical culture and an appreciation of new cultural emphases. Thomas Aquinas put his blessing on trends by casting his *Summa* in Aristotelian mold.

As we know, the Dark Ages were displaced by better times, and the world headed gloriously for the

Facts, Myths and Maybes

Renaissance. To be sure the Renaissance was a big price to pay for the centuries of darkness, but for those keeping scorecards, if the church is to be held accountable for the one, it merits plaudits for the other.

* * *

The Inquisition had redeeming features. It helped secular courts bring criminals to justice, for instance, and it preserved Spain and the Spanish Americas from the Protestant reformers.

RUBBISH . . . The Inquisition had no redeeming features, and to argue so is to strain all logic. One might just as well try to justify the Inquisition because it was the church's baby, so to speak. Which, incidentally, has been attempted, even in this century. A cardinal of Pius X's curia, Allesio Maria Lépicier, braved the thought: "The naked fact that the church, of her own authority, has tried heretics and condemned them to be delivered to death, shows that she truly has the right of killing . . . [W]ho dares to say that the church has erred in a matter so grave as this?"

Well, just about everyone. The Inquisition, a reign of terror that extended over several centuries in varying degrees of intensity, stands as one of the shabbiest chapters of church history. The wonder for some is that it could ever have occurred in an institution based on love, understanding and forgiveness. But it did and, as noted, it was hardly a momentary aberration. The Inquisition was long the church's ultimate weapon against those who disagreed with it.

The Inquisition began in 1229 in Southern France, when Pope Gregory IX (1227-1241) extended existing local legislation against heretics, including liability of death, and incorporated the process into a papal tribunal headed by the Dominicans. (The Franciscans were brought along later.) Pope Innocent IV (1243-1254) refined the office and its tasks with the promulgation in 1252 of *Ad extirpanda,* a bull authorizing use of torture to secure proof of heresy. With *Ad extirpanda* the Inquisition was under full sail.

In establishing the Inquisition, the church initially was reacting to Albigensian and Waldensian challenges—such as denial of the existence of Purgatory; the doubtful efficacy of votive offerings and of Masses for the dead; the questioning of the validity of sacraments performed by so-called bad priests; and presumptuous claims of the laity, men and women, to preach. Eventually, as we shall see, the grounds were expanded to cover all manner of supposed human transgression.

Inquisition tactics included systematic interrogation, use of the rack, solitary confinement and imprisonment—followed, in cases of the unrepentant and unabsolved, by confiscation of property and finally death, usually by burning at the stake, although some were hanged. (Because the church did not shed blood, those condemned to death were turned over to the secular arm.) Horror stories abound of the Inquisition's terrors.

The Inquisition spared England and Germany, but it lasted in France into the sixteenth century, and it resonated in Italy, if only in name, as late as 1965, when at last the Curia department known as the Holy Office of the Inquisition was renamed the Congregation for the Doctrine of the Faith.

It was in Spain and the Spanish colonies, however, that the Inquisition was especially cruel and long-lasting. The Spanish tribunal was set up in 1478 during the reign of Ferdinand the Catholic and Queen Isabella, who considered the faith in Spain threatened by alleged pseudo-converts from Judaism (*Maranos*) and Islam (*Moriscos*).

The first Grand Inquisitor of the Spanish Inquisition was the infamous Dominican, Tomás de Torquemada. Thousands of Jews went to the stake as ''impenitent sinners'' under Torquemada, and history records him as instrumental in the banishment of Jews from Spain in 1492. Those who stayed behind were hardly better off, for Torquemada passed beyond heresy and brought under the Inquisition civil offenses such as polygamy, bigamy, impersonation of priests, forgery, perjury, etc. He was such a scourge and his evil so far reaching—in time the Spanish Inquisition reached Mexico, Lima and Cartegena—that the name Torquemada became synonymous with cruelty.

The Inquisition petered out, albeit slowly. Its dying gasp was in the early nineteenth century, when it was revived in Spain in conjunction with an effort to restore royal absolutism. The Inquisition's last victim is recorded there: a village schoolmaster; hanged in 1826.

* * *

Certainly the Crusades had redeeming features. They quickened religious engergies, broadened East-West horizons, and stimulated economic and cultural contacts between western Christianity and the Byzantine and Islamic worlds.

PERHAPS . . . But so what? On balance the Crusades were negatives, and they left a legacy of hate, enmity and suspicion that exist to this day. Note, for instance, how quick many in the East were to frame the Persian Gulf war of 1991 in the context of another "holy" Crusade from the West, this one in the cause of oil. No, the Crusades—the Fourth Crusade especially— were anything but church picnics. With the Inquisition, they must be accounted barbaric, among the great misadventures of Christian history.

A long misadventure they were. The Crusades stretched over 200 years, beginning in 1097 when Pope Urban II (1088-1099) called for the freeing of Jerusalem and the rescuing of the Holy Land from the infidel, and sent a slaughtering army of between 150,000 and 300,000 off to the East with promises of indulgences, remission of sin, and eternal glory in heaven. Like those who would follow, the crusaders were often murderers, ravagers and plunderers before they were Christians on a so-called holy enterprise.

There were eight Crusades in all, and successively they dominated East-West history until the fall of Acre in 1291, the event which effectively ended a formal western Christian presence in the East. For all the bloodshed and the anguish of those two centuries, the western church had nothing to show that elementary diplomacy could not have been expected to accomplish—including, eventually, visiting rights to the holy places.

As for the Fourth Crusade, it took place in 1204 and by Venetian ingenuity was deflected from an attack against Egypt to one against Constantinople, one of civilization's greatest cities and seat of an empire. Constantinople fell on April 12, and immediately there began an orgy of plundering and ravagement that shames history. Masterpieces of antiquity were stolen or destroyed. Churches were sacked, and clerics vied with knights in competition for priceless relics. The hallowed church of St. Sophia itself became the scene of bloody and sacrilegious orgies. Finally, the empire itself was carved up and divided among the chief secular players. The Crusade had turned political with consequences that would extend over centuries.

A footnote to this chapter of history:

The Crusades of the East had an afterlife elsewhere in the world, becoming the inspiration and model for holy wars against heretics and heathens. The *Conquistadores* went to the New World thinking of themselves as auxiliaries of the Crusades, and a sixteenth-century war in Hungary rang of the Crusades. Obsessed by the idea of the Crusades, popes considered launching them against schismatic sects closer to home. But times had changed, and there was also the industriousness of the Inquisition.

* * *

The Children's Crusade belongs to mythology.

ANYTHING BUT . . . The Children's Crusade is not included in the role of the eight Crusades, but there was one and it brims with pathos.

It took place in 1212, between the Fourth and Fifth Crusades, and was spearheaded by a shepherd boy named Stephen from Vendome, France, and a German child from Cologne named Nicolas. Separately the youths envisioned Jerusalem being liberated by a miracle worked by young innocents, and as boy preachers they rallied thousands to the effort. Stephen

Facts, Myths and Maybes

rode by wagon southward to Marseilles, promising his legion of thousands that the seas would part for them, as they had for Moses, so that they could march dryshod to the Holy Land. Nicolas took his followers southward through Italy to Brindisi, gathering recruits as he moved along, their numbers eventually reaching 20,000.

Of course, the whole thing was a fiasco. The seas didn't part for Stephen, and his crusaders fell victim to exhaustion, disease and slave traders, thousands being sold to the Moors in Egypt. As for Nicolas' legion, it achieved nothing, ending as echo in the medieval folk legend of the Pied Piper of Hamelin, later turned to poetry by Robert Browning.

Disaster begot disaster, for Pope Innocent III (1198-1216) used the inspiration of the children to launch another full-blown Crusade. "The very children put us to shame," he wrote; "while we sleep they go forth gladly to conquer the Holy Land." At the Fourth Lateran Council (1215), therefore, he proclaimed a Crusade for 1217. Never before had a Crusade been proclaimed through a general council, so there were unusually pious hopes for its success. The Crusade was to proceed to the Holy Land through Egypt. It never got beyond Cairo.

* * *

267

John Deedy

The church once forbade priests and religious to practice medicine or surgery.

FACT . . . Once upon a time clerics and religious, sisters and brothers, were indeed forbidden to practice medicine or surgery. However, what was once a flat-out prohibition has given way in recent times, first to permission to practice through apostolic indult, and more recently an arrangement that leaves the apostolic indult unmandated, but presumes an understanding that clerics will avoid practices that are ''alien'' to the clerical state.

What made the practice of medicine and surgery by clerics ''alien'' in the first place was (1) the fundamental principle that the church did not shed blood (hence, as noted earlier, the turning over of the condemned to the secular arm in days when heretics were executed), and (2) concern that a patient might die or incur a mutilation (loss of a principal member of the body) as a result of the cleric's ministrations. In context of the latter, no matter that an amputation might be a medical necessity. Secular physicians could perform the procedure, as the canonical statute did not apply to them. But a cleric could not, since ''cutting''—''burning'' as well—were outlawed by church law for all in the clerical state.

Indeed, where clerics were concerned it did not matter that the patient's death might be accidental or that the amputation (mutilation) was unforeseen—in other words, a medical necessity developing from the patient's condition. For clerics even no-fault or unwitting departure from the norm was enough under any circumstances for them to incur an "irregularity"—that is, an impediment impeding the cleric's exercise of Holy Orders. The impediment could be lifted, but only by competent ecclesiastical authority.

All this was very ironic, for popes were strong patrons of the medical sciences, and over the centuries many of medicine's greatest advances were credited to Catholic hospitals and the science departments of universities with ecclesiastical charters. Nonetheless, as early as 1219 Pope Honorius III (1212-1227) forbade all clerics not just to practice, but even to study medicine, lest their vocations be jeopardized by their being plunged into worldly cares and environments.

Four years before, Lateran Council IV (1215) had ruled that "no subdeacon, deacon or priest [may] exercise any art of medicine which involves cutting or burning," so by the time Honorius acted, the point was clear. As the 1913 *Catholic Encyclopedia* worded it, for men of the cloth ". . . it [was] preferable to study theology and become physicians of souls rather than to cure bodies, which is a secular profession."

Of course there were always exceptions. Priests who possessed a knowledge of medicine were serving as "physicians-in-ordinary" to princes as late as the fifteenth century, and in the absence of secular doctors, clerics could practice medicine through medical necessity or out of "pity and charity towards the poor," though in no instance were the clerics to accept payment for their services. Aware of the health realities of mission lands, Clement XII (1730-1740) issued the bull *Cum sicut* allowing clerics to practice medicine there, although again services had to be gratis and the clerics were to abstain from cutting and burning. Also, they were required to withdraw from practice, if and when there were sufficient numbers of secular physicians on hand to care for the sick.

The United States was no exception. The Second Council of Baltimore of 1866, invoking Pope Benedict XIV (1740-1758), barred to clerics the practice of medicine and surgery, making no exceptions for charitable or gratis services, presumably because there were sufficient numbers of secular doctors about. The only way around the prohibition was by apostolic indult; that is, special permission from the Holy See to deviate from the common law of the church.

These prohibitions and restrictions extended to religious women as well, of course, but were eased in 1936 by *Constans ac sedula,* a decree approving the study and practice of medicine for medical sisters with public vows. Helping dictate the accommodation were cultural traditions in parts of the world that forbade women to see male doctors. Women religious had to be trained in medicine, if in many mission lands the latest in professional medical care was to be available to women living there. *Constans ac sedula* gave great impetus to religious orders such as Medical Missionary Sisters and the Medical Missionaries of Mary.

As for Canon Law, the prohibition was specific in the 1917 code. Canon 139, section 2, stated that the practice of medicine and surgery, while not unbecoming, was alien to the clerical state, and therefore clerics were to practice neither profession without an apostolic indult: *Sine apostolico indulto medicinam vel chirurgiam ne exerceant.* . . .

The new 1983 code does not repeat that provision. How much is changed, therefore?

The elimination of the provision would make it seem that an apostolic indult is no longer required by general church law for properly trained clerics to practice either medicine or surgery. (Psychiatry too, it being a form of modern medicine.) On the other hand, it is noted that Canon 285, section 2, of the new code states that clerics (including permanent deacons) are ''to avoid those things which, although not unbecoming, are nevertheless alien to the clerical state.'' Since this phrase was used in the introductory section of Canon 139 of the 1917 code, some feel the case can be made that clerics still need an indult to practice medicine and surgery.

Similarly, question lingers in some minds about the

force of the Council of Baltimore provision (#153). Since it is not contrary but only more extensive than the 1983 Code of Canon Law, some say the argument could be made that it has the force of law, so that in the U.S. if nowhere else, an apostolic indult is still required.

A check with the Office of Canonical Affairs of the National Conference of Catholic Bishops in Washington, D.C., elicited the contrary opinion that, while some dioceses may have policies of their own, the old prohibition against clerical practice of medicine and surgery does not apply in universal law, since it is not explicitly mentioned in the new Code of Canon Law.

* * *

The Shroud of Turin is an embarrassment that the church is anxious to bury in the memory.

SEEMINGLY NOT . . . It will be remembered that when the Shroud of Turin was exposed as a fraud in 1988, following extensive carbon-14 tests on fragments of the cloth by independent scientists at three different laboratories, Catholics were encouraged to continue their veneration of the shroud as a powerful pictorial image of Christ. Then, in 1990 Vatican spokesperson Joaquin Navarro-Valls announced that the shroud could be subjected to additional scientific testing to determine its origin and possible use as the burial cloth of the crucified Christ. Two years later nothing had

Facts, Myths and Maybes

happened, so it could be that the statements, the second especially, were made to console or reassure the devout. On the other hand, the statements could also indicate a reluctance in Rome to accept the findings of fraud. The church, of course, never formally claimed the shroud as a relic of Christ's crucifixion, but still no one likes to be made the fool.

Rome shouldn't feel abashed. The Shroud of Turin—a cloth about thirteen-and-a-half feet long and four-and-a-quarter feet wide, bearing bloodstains and a faint brownish image front and back of a crucified five-foot, eleven-inch Caucasian weighing about 178 pounds—fooled a lot of people for a long time.

The shroud first came to light in mid-fourteenth century in the possession of a famous French knight named Geoffrey de Charny. Geoffrey acquired the cloth sometime before 1356, but how no one knows. Did he receive it as stolen property, and therefore could not reveal its provenance? Was Geoffrey part of a conspiracy to fool and defraud? History is full of such instances, right through to William Dawson and Piltdown Man in our century. No one knows, for Geoffrey de Charny died at Potiers in 1356 defending his king, John II (Jean le Bon), in battle against English invaders. His secret died with him.

The Shroud of Turin has had such a checkered career that is is difficult to figure the emotion invested in it. For one thing, there are the rival shrouds of Besancon,

John Deedy

Cadouin, Champiegne and Xabregas, among other places, all of them similarly impressed with allegedly crucified figures. For another, there is the testimony of the Bishop of Troyes, where Geoffrey de Charny lived and where his shroud was displayed in the church at Lirey; in 1389 the bishop appealed to Clement VII, the Avignon Claimant, to stop the nonsense surrounding the shroud, on grounds it was the work of an artist who some years before had confessed to painting it. Finally, there is papal history; beginning with Clement VII, the tradition was to describe the shroud as a "representation," not necessarily the real thing. So why the big fuss over the 1988 findings?

Or, how come this cloth is known as the Shroud of Turin, when its origins are so French? Because in 1578, the shroud was transferred from Lirey to Turin, in Italy, where it is enshrined in the cathedral. In 1933 it was placed on public view, and then again in 1978, at which time the intensive scientific studies were begun that dated the shroud between 1260 and 1390, therefore at most 728 years old.

The shroud, which had been in the possession of the House of Savoy, was willed to Pope John Paul II in 1983.

End of story . . . maybe.

* * *

Facts, Myths and Maybes

Yes, Virginia, there is a Santa Claus, and his real name is Saint Nicholas.

MYTH . . . Saint Nicholas is commonly associated with Santa Claus, but it's an inaccurate association. Santa Claus is a legend of pagan or pre-Christian origin, based on the folklore of Thor, the god of fire in Germanic mythology, who in turn was associated with winter and the yule log, and who rode about in a cart drawn not by reindeer but by goats named Cracker and Gnasher.

The Saint Nicholas/Santa Claus association was introduced into America by Protestants, but not the Pilgrims and Puritans of New England; they were a stern lot who didn't even observe Christmas. The popularizers, rather, were the Dutch of New Amsterdam, what we know now as New York. Their ancestors had converted Saint Nicholas of Myra, a bona fide fourth-century bishop celebrated for his generosity, into a Nordic magician dashing about in a sleigh loaded with presents, his name transformed in the process from Saint Nicholas to Sint Klaes, and only a lisp away from Santa Claus. The introduction of his tale into our lore is credited to Bret Harte, the famed story-teller of California's nineteenth-century '49ers; he happened to be of Dutch-English parentage.

As for the real Saint Nicholas, he died around 350. His fame as a gift-giver was such that in 1087 zealots stole his bones and whisked them from Asia Minor to Bari in southern Italy, where they were relocated as the focus of a major shrine. Theft has its rewards. Churches by the hundreds were suddenly being dedicated to Saint Nicholas throughout western Europe, and by the thirteenth century the devout were marking his feast day as a day of gift-giving. That day wasn't December 25, though. It was December 6. That's still Saint Nicholas' feast day. You can look it up.

* * *

Christ was born on December 25.

POSSIBLY . . . although the odds are 365-to-1 that he wasn't. The fact is no one knows for sure the exact day on which Christ was born. The Gospels are of no help; indeed, they offer data that contradict rather than support a December date for Christ's birth. For instance, a census putting thousands of families on the road during the Mideast's winter weather would have been most unlikely, even by Roman standards of insensitivity. Also, winter being the rainy season, it is unlikely that shepherds would have been tending their sheep by night; the sheep would not have been exposed to December's rains and cold nights; they'd have been in shelters.

Several theories exist on how December 25 came to be observed as Christ's birthday, the most common being that the early Fathers acted to co-opt the Roman civil holiday of Mithra, the Unconquered Sun, *Natalis Invicti,* patron of the imperial army. Because the Roman feast was occasioned by the winter solstice, the observance of Christmas could thus be said to have been governed more by the distance of the sun from the celestial equator than by any message from angels singing from on high—more, that is, by the sun entering the sign of Capricorn than by a star fixing itself above a stable in Bethlehem on a particular calendar day. Invocations of Christ as the Unconquered and of the Sun of Justice fed the Mithra association, but Pope Leo I (440-461) reproved that association lest it encourage a cult of sun worship.

On the other hand, there was more pious theory linking the date of Christ's birth to the Feast of the Annunciation and the Archangel Gabriel's announcement to Mary that she was to be the mother of God. The Annunciation was observed on March 25, and counting nine months from that date, presto, one arrived at December 25. The trouble here is that latterday scholars were not able to trace the March 25 observance of the Annunciation back to the fourth century, by which time the observance of Christ's birth on December 25 was well entrenched. Rome was observing December 25 as Christ's birthday before the year 354, and by 395 that calendar date had been adopted as well in the East. Accordingly, it is more likely that the

277

Annunication's date was determined by Christmas, not vice versa.

The whole discussion is long since academic, of course. For one reason or another, December 25 came to be known as Christmas, and so it is observed today. But Christmas could just as easily have been set on July 4. Now wouldn't that have complicated family barbecues in the U.S.?

* * *

The story of the Magi or Three Wise Men is just as problematical as the date of Christ's birth.

YES & NO . . . Mark, Luke and John are silent on the subject, but we know from Matthew (2:2-11) that there were Magi or Wise Men, and that from somewhere in the East they followed a star "till it came and stood over where the young child was." But that's about all that is known with certainty. Indeed, how many Magi there were is anyone's guess. In the East, tradition favors twelve; the West settled on three, figuring that since three gifts were presented (gold, frankincense and myrrh), it is logical that each was brought by a single person. As for the names of the three Magi— Gaspar, Melchior and Balthasar—they belong to a late tradition and are not regarded as authentic.

But, wait, that's not all.

Chances are that the Holy Family was long gone from

the stable at Bethlehem by the time the Magi arrived. In fact, little Jesus might have been as much as one or two years old before he was visited by the Magi. This is because the Magi likely started out from Persia or Arabia (one school holds for Babylon), and thus would have had to travel a distance of 1000 to 1200 miles, a distance that could have taken anywhere from several months to a year by camel, to say nothing of preparation time.

Finally, that celestial sign the Magi followed may not have been a star. It may really have been a comet spun off by a remarkable conjunction of Jupiter and Saturn that scientists say occurred in the year 7 B.C., or of Jupiter and Venus the next year.

But what's the difference: comet or star; Bethlehem or Galilee as the place of visitation? The Magi got there, didn't they?

* * *

Unlike Christmas, Easter is a movable feast, meaning it can occur almost any springtime Sunday.

FACT . . . Any feast which has a variable observance date is a movable feast, and Easter, which is marked on the first Sunday following the first full moon of spring, can occur as early as March 22 or as late as April 25. The Sundays of Advent and the observance of the Ascension, Pentecost and Corpus Christi are other examples of movable feasts. Their place on the liturgical calendar is distinct from fixed or immovable feasts, which always occur on the same date—like Christmas on December 25, as noted, and the Circumcision, now called the Feast of the Solemnity of Mary the Mother of God, on January 1.

Agreement on the observance of Easter was not reached until the Council of Nicaea in 325, but acceptance was far from unanimous—and indeed it's far from unanimous now, most Eastern churches marking Easter according to liturgical calendars of their own. The variance between East and West reflects the incomplete settlement of the so-called Easter Controversy of the early church; namely, what was the proper time for observing Easter?

The Easter-Controversy debate centered first on the licitness of celebrating Easter on a weekday, a possibility ruled out by tradition from earliest Christian times that Christ rose on the first day of the week, Sunday. That agreed on, the question became, which Sunday? Nicaea decreed that Easter Sunday must follow the fourteenth day of the paschal moon, and that paschal moon was to be the moon whose fourteenth day followed the spring equinox. The problem was that churches using the Roman calendar and respectful of certain Jewish customs opted for a date derivative of the Jewish observance of the Pasch, or Passover. Difficulties were further complicated because East and West did not calculate by uniform lunar cycles. Rome itself adopted and discarded several cycles in attempting to arrive at a more accurate determination of Easter, before adopting the tables of Dionysius Exiguus and the Metonic cycle in 525.

Differences were never fully resolved between all the churches, but the point is not one of contention between East and West. Agreement is general that the date of Easter is not a dogmatic issue, much less one of astronomical science, but only a matter of ecclesiastical and social convenience—and now, of course, tradition.

* * *

Halloween is at heart a religious tradition.

MYTH . . . Halloween is rather a pagan tradition, although as with other pagan holidays, an effort was made to Christianize it once the church was in the ascendancy.

Actually the only thing religious about Halloween is its name, deriving from the English term for the Feast of All Saints, November 1. In Middle English usage, the feast was that of All Hallows, from the word "hallow," meaning to make or honor as holy. The eve of All Hallows being a special, indeed festive occasion, October 31 evening telescoped in time to Halloween.

Ancient Romans celebrated October 31 as the festival

281

of Pomona, goddess of gardens. Ancient Celts knew the day as "Samhain," or "end of summer," and observed it as the end of the food-growing season, and year's end as well. Thus once upon a time in Ireland, Wales, Scotland and Brittany the following day, November 1, was New Year's.

The Celts also believed that ghosts visited the earth on Samhain, and so they built bonfires (fires made with bones for fuel) to scare them away. When the Celts were christianized, they joined with other Christian groups in an effort to appropriate the festival and transfer it to the eve of All Souls Day, November 2. The shift seemed logical given Samhain's association with the dead, but the effort was unsuccessful.

As for the modern trick-or-treat custom, it seems to come from the Celtic belief that those ghosts who roamed the earth on Samhain were full of mischief, and that the surest way to be free of their shenanigans was to treat them. The ghosts could also be foiled by dressing and acting like them, hence the donning of Halloween costumes.

* * *

There was never any such practice as "boy-bishoping."

WRONG . . . "Boy-bishoping" was a custom in the Middle Ages in England, Germany and other countries. The custom centered about the Feasts of Saint

Facts, Myths and Maybes

Nicholas (December 6) and of the Holy Innocents (December 28), and involved the playful elevation of a young boy to the rank of bishop. The boy was dressed as a bishop, complete to miter and crozier, provided with attendants, and sometimes actually invested with authority. Depending on the place, he might preside at ceremonies and offices (Mass excluded), preach, bless people, convey patronage and make appointments. He even had a Latin title—in fact several: *episcopus puerorum, episcopus innocentium,* or if elected from the cathedral school or choir, *episcopus scholariorum* or *episcopus chorestarum.*

In Britain, the custom related to the so-called Feast of Fools, a quasi-religious festival devised as a counterpart to a secular festival headed by a Lord of Misrule, and traceable ultimately to the Saturnalia of ancient Rome.

The problem for the church was that fun turned to burlesque, including on the Continent. There was great play, for instance, on Balaam's ass, the talking animal of Numbers 22:21ff. In Rouen, a priest capered about and uttered prophesies from a hollow wooden effigy of an ass, while at Beauvais the rubrics of the Mass included braying by the celebrant, the people responding "Hee-haw, Hee-haw, Hee-haw." There were other extravagances, such as vespers being sung in falsetto, followed by feasting, fun and dancing.

The lark had carried too far. In 1210 Pope Innocent

John Deedy

III (1198-1216) finally cracked down, forbidding aspects of the Feast of Fools, especially the lampooning of priests, deacons and subdeacons. In 1246 Innocent IV (1243-1254) added the penalty of excommunication for disobeying the prohibition. It was not until 1431, however, that "boy-bishoping" was outlawed, the action being taken by the Council of Basle. None of the practices seems to have died quickly though. Succeeding decades saw the condemnations renewed time and again, evidence that fiat did not easily separate Catholics of the time from frolic. But then came the Reformation, and the time for high-jinks was over. The frolicking came to an end.

The curious thing was that, whether out of naivete or innocence, the masses of people were not embarrassed by the larks, much less offended. Of course, no intentional element of contempt was involved, so there was no popular outcry even when the festivities crossed into the profane—as happened when altars came to be used for banquet tables, and for rolling dice and playing cards. For Catholics of the time, the whole business appears to have been nothing more than variations of the modern Mardi Gras in places like New Orleans and Rio de Janeiro.

Still, the high-jinks would come back to haunt, for "boy-bishoping" and the Feast of Fools would become additional weapons against the Roman church in the hands of the Reformers. Sir Walter Scott made this clear

Facts, Myths and Maybes

in his 1820 novel *The Abbot,* dealing with Mary Queen of Scots' imprisonment in Lochleven Castle, her escape and flight to England after the battle of Langside. One of the book's episodes has Protestants intruding on Mass at the Abbey of Kennaquhair and demanding that the monks substitute in its stead the revels of the Feast of Fools.

*   *   *

The world reckons time by Catholic Christian calculations.

TRUE . . . The centuries and years before and after Christ's birth are traditionally designated B.C. and A.D.—the B.C. standing for "before Christ," and the A.D. for *Anno Domini,* Latin for "year of Our Lord." Accordingly, our century is the twentieth A.D., and our times the 1990s A.D. There are exceptions, however. Jewish people keep their own calendar, and for reasons both ecumenical and secular there's a growing tendency among many people to drop B.C. and A.D. for the designates B.C.E. and C.E.—"before the Common Era" and "Common Era," respectively.

More oblique, but just as surely Catholic Christian as the designation for years is the calendar of months and days by which life is regulated universally—or almost universally. Ethiopia follows what is known as the Julian Calendar. But for the rest of the world, the norm is the Gregorian Calendar, the spectacular achievement of the reign of Pope Gregory XIII (1572-1585).

The Julian Calendar was devised in Roman times, taking its name from the Emperor Caius Julius Caesar. There was tinkering over the years with this calendar, but essentially it was calendar devising a year of 365-1/4 days, divided into 12 months, the months containing the same number of days as our own after August was fitted with 31 days at Augustus Caesar's insistence. After all, the month was named in his honor (August/ Augustus), and how could his month have fewer days than the month that honored Julius Caesar (July/ Julius)?

The Julian Calendar was an enormous advance over anything that existed to date, but it was still a "slow" calendar—so slow, in fact, that by the sixteenth century the calendar year was running ten days behind the sun. Scientists were exasperated, and so were churchmen. Several church councils, including Trent (1563), urged action to correct the situation, the church being interested because the imprecise calendar was playing tricks with liturgical schedules.

Nineteen years after Trent, the puzzle of the slow calendar was solved. Gregory XIII was pope, and credit for the breakthrough went to the scholars Lilius, Clavius and Chacon (Chaconius). Key to their solution was the simple rearrangement of leap years to offset the difference between the common year (365 days) and the astronomical year (365-1/4 days), then in order to catch up to the sun, a jumping ahead of the calendar by eleven days. Upon acceptance, October 4, 1582 was thus followed by October 15, 1582. Perfect, but not quite. The Gregorian Calendar still exceeds the true astronomical year by 26 seconds, but it will be 35 centuries before that difference amounts to a day.

Initially, the world divided along denominational lines in accepting the Gregorian Calendar. Catholic countries were quick to adopt the new calendar, but not countries influenced by churches of the Reformation. England, for instance, did not accept the Gregorian Calendar until 1751. For reasons all its own, Russia held out until this century, with the curious historical footnote that the famous October Revolution of 1917 actually took place in November, 1917. Today the world's largely in line, although if you're going to Addis Ababa, you'd better set your calendar back eleven days.

* * *

Bells and their melodies are replete with Christian religious meaning.

FACT . . . Bells are full of Christian symbolism, including perhaps the most famous bell of all—that which rings from the Victoria Clock Tower of London's House of Parliament. Originally fitted to the clock of

John Deedy

the University Church, St. Mary's the Great, Cam-
bridge, its quarter-hour and hourly chimes are known
worldwide, ringing from mighty bell towers to parlor
grandfather clocks. The chimes speak a silent invocation:

> Lord, through this hour,
> Be thou our guide;
> So by thy power;
> No foot shall slide.

Bells have existed from time immemorial, of course.
The ancient Romans used them to summon people to
public baths and to processions. They were also used
to signal alarms: invasions, fires, etc. The church
adopted their use around the fourth or fifth century,
initially putting them to practical usages, such as the
rousing of monks from their cells and the calling of the
faithful for church services. The first ecclesial application is said to have been by Paulinus, Bishop of Nola,
about the year 400.

The ringing of bells took on elaborate religious usages
in the Middle Ages. There was the ''sacrament bell,''
announcing the celebration of the Eucharist (a custom
preserved in some places with the tinkling of a bell at
the elevation of the host and the chalice during the
Eucharistic Prayer); the ''sermon bell,'' giving notice
that a sermon was about to be preached (especially
necessary in large cathedrals before the advent of

public-address systems); and inevitably a "passing bell," tolled on deaths or funerals (in the pious belief that the sound of a consecrated bell drove off demons, who lurked ready to waylay the departing soul). A hierarchy of symbolism was attached to the "passing bell," its being rung twice for a woman, three times for a man, and a greater number of times for a cleric, the exact number depending on the cleric's honors and position. (Does one detect a note of chauvinism and clerical elitism in that arrangement?)

With the flowering of Marian devotions, bells were increasingly dedicated to Mary, and rung in the evening as a signal for the saying of three Hail Marys. These became known as "Ave bells," and the prayer they encouraged grew into the famous Angelus devotion dating from the thirteenth century.

There were, however, interesting variations to the "Ave bells." In England, a strong devotional cult existed to Gabriel, the angel who announced to Mary that she would give birth to Jesus, and so a number of bells were dedicated to him, called "Gabriel bells" naturally. Bells were also dedicated to Jesus, Peter, John, Magdalene, Augustine and Raphael, among others, most with Latin or vernacular inscriptions in their castings associating their sounds with prayer; e.g., "This emblem of Peter is struck in the name of Christ" (Bedfordshire, England); "I am the voice of life; I call you come and pray" (Strasbourg); and the principal bell of St. Peter's in Rome, which rings in the name of the Mother of the Lord, and of Peter and Paul, *In nomine Domini Matris, Petrique, Paulique,* etc.

Many of the old bells are gone, the victims of religious or political reform, or of warfare. The Strasbourg bell just cited was taken down at the time of the French Revolution, and the bell of Rouen's cathedral was melted down in 1793—although surprisingly the inscription on the Rouen bell turned out to be whimsical rather than religious. It read: *Je suis George d'Ambois/Qui trente cinque mille pois;/Mais lui qui me pesera/Trente six mille me trouvera*—"I am George d'Ambois, weighing 35,000 pounds, but he who weighs me will find 36,000."

* * *

Church bells, like people, were once actually baptized.

VIRTUALLY . . . Church bells acquired pedigrees and personalities, being given names and accorded voices. More to the point, they were christened in a ceremony known as the "baptism of the bells." In Catholic understanding, the "voice" with which the bells "spoke" and the "baptism" that put them into service were metaphorical terms. For others, however, the whole business was problematical, so much so that the ritual known as the "baptism of the bells" became the subject of serious theological controversy in the sixteenth century. Martin Luther led the objectors, claiming the ritual smacked of superstition and of profanation of the actual sacrament of baptism. He spoke for Protestant reformers generally.

The objectors had a strong point, for the ritual did indeed closely parallel that of the sacrament of baptism. The bells were exorcised, and water, salt and unctions came into play. Individual bells, as noted in the previous entry, were given names, and an engraved inscription proclaimed a holy mission, sometimes in the first person singular; e.g., the main bell in the bell tower at Boston College: "I am Ignatius of Loyola./ I arouse all the faithful unto seeking the greater glory of God / Throughout the years. / The League of the Sacred Heart of Jesus donated me."

That's not all. In the course of the christening, the bells were incensed. They were washed inside and out, and dried with white towels. Psalms were recited, and the bells were then signed with the oil of the sick, seven places on the outside and four on the inside. The formal blessing came as the celebrants intoned the following words, with accompanying signs of the cross: "May this bell be + hallowed, O Lord, and + consecrated in the name of the + Father, and of the + Son, and of the + Holy Ghost. In honor of Saint (name). Peace be to thee." There were more prayers, more incensing, and then the reading of the Gospel passage concerning Martha and Mary.

John Deedy

It was a mighty elaborate ceremony, and that confusion should exist between the blessing of a bell and a baptism is readily apparent.

Luther, however, was not the first to be bothered by the similarities. Back in the ninth century Charlemagne was so troubled by the bells' ceremony as to order in his *Capitularies* that no bell be baptized (*ut cloccas non baptizent*). Still the old ways prevailed. In 1851 Longfellow would speak of bells being baptized in *The Golden Legend:* ''For these bells have been anointed/ And baptized with holy water.'' And even as late as 1913 the Gilmary Society's *Catholic Encyclopedia* was offering the centuries-old ritual protested by Charlemagne and Luther as the liturgically correct way to christen or bless bells; the ritual outlined in the previous paragraphs is from that encyclopedia.

The Catholic rejoinder to all objections was that the resemblances between the ritual for the blessing of bells and for the sacrament of baptism were superficial, and the term ''baptism of bells'' was used only in a popular sense. Officials further pointed out that in the blessing of bells, the use of water was separate from the form (the actual words of dedication). Liturgically speaking, the distinction was an important one, since sacramental relevance rests in the combination of the two actions. In the sacrament of baptism, water and words are used together and comprise the very essence of the sacrament.

Facts, Myths and Maybes

The church's position, in sum, was that the christening of a church bell was not particularly different from the christening of a ship on launching. As for the washing of the bell, that equated to the washing of the altar in the old Holy Thursday ritual, nothing more. If the bells' ritual of blessing still seemed imitative of the sacrament of baptism, so what? Many of the church's ceremonials were imitative. The rite for the blessing of palms, for instance, followed the arrangement of the Mass; the rite for the coronation of kings followed that of the consecration of a bishop. (The last wasn't a particularly felicitous example, as some kings did confuse the two rituals and come eventually to think of themselves as spiritual personalities with episcopal powers.)

In any instance, the bells' controversy belongs to another day. The old ritual was in place for twelve centuries, but the current one is far simpler and less associative with a sacrament, baptism or any other. As contained in the *Book of Blessings* of the Roman Ritual, 1989 edition, the ritual calls for prayers, readings and intercessions, but the exorcisms are eliminated, as well as the washing. The ritual does allow, ''as circumstances suggest,'' for a sprinkling of the bells with holy water and for their incensing; if employed, this takes place between the prayer of blessing and the recitation of Psalm 149 (''Sing to the Lord a new song, etc.''). But there's no parodying of the ritual for baptism, and

293

nothing anymore even approximating the form (words) of baptism.

* * *

The church is an anti-intellectual institution.

NO & MAYBE . . . It is impossible to believe that a church that produced a Mozart, a Michelangelo, a Pasteur, a Rouault and, on the level of saintliness and social consciousness, a Francis of Assisi, could even remotely be considered anti-intellectual. On the other hand, there was the repudiation of Galileo and, among other things, the unreal notion that interest charged on money lent was a form of usury and therefore immoral; neither science nor modern economic theory could begin to exist on premises that contributed to those ill-formed decisions. So, yes, there are proud chapters of history, but there are likewise skeletons in the Catholic closet.

Of course, too, there is Freudian theory that belief itself is an anti-intellectual exercise, a form of delusion—which, if accepted, would make all churches anti-intellectual, not just the Catholic Church. All believers reject that supposition, but it's not what we're talking about here anyway.

Our question: Is the Catholic Church anti-intellectual?

That's a question that generates more questions,

some akin to those posed initially. Could an institution that produced a monastic tradition so steeped as the Catholic one in the arts and sciences be anti-intellectual? And what of an institution that has produced worldwide so respected an educational system, from the elementary to the university levels; could it be anti-intellectual? The questions seem to answer themselves.

Matters of the minds have always been central to Catholicism. Nonetheless, mistakes along the way subverted certain matters of the mind for periods long or short to considerations of orthodoxy and maintenance of the status quo, with consequences that often required Catholics to live in two separate worlds of intellect—one of orthodoxy, the other of impartial scholarship.

American Catholics of a given age may know these separate worlds better than Catholics elsewhere, for until the latter 1960s those separate worlds clearly existed in the United States, to the detriment of Catholic intellectual standing. It was a situation that resulted finally in deep soul-searching, and debate over whether American Catholics had defaulted on their intellectual heritage.

The debate was sparked in the 1950s by Monsignor John Tracy Ellis of the Catholic University of America and Father John J. Cavanaugh of the University of Notre Dame. Separately they suggested that American

John Deedy

Catholics were remiss in upholding the intellectual traditions of the church, and that this phenomenon placed the American church in inferior position to other churches, notably in Western Europe. The question was put most starkly by Cavanaugh. "Where," he asked, "are the Catholic Salks, Oppenheimers, Einsteins?"

The American Catholic press, traditionally the instinctive defender of orthodoxy, cried foul, interpreting Cavanaugh's query as a slur on Catholic schools and, to lesser extent, on the priesthood itself. Apropos the latter, what more learned body as a whole could be found, one Catholic-press editorialist wanted to know, than the American priesthood? (It turned out, not surprisingly, that the editorialist was a priest.) A less emotional, if not entirely elucidating perspective was provided by Cardinal John Wright, then Bishop of Worcester, Massachusetts, in a prefatory note to Ellis' book on the subject, *American Catholics and the Intellectual Life* (1956).

"What we have called the 'great debate' raging here in the United States at the moment is doubtless no more than a phase within our own land of an argument that has been going on in Europe for decades," Wright wrote. "Traditionally, the European intellectual has been acknowledged by his contemporaries, even those who might disagree with him, to have a 'vocation' beyond the limits of his own profession of writing or science or teaching. It is a vocation quite apart from that of the functionary or representative of church or of state, and it has obvious and grave perils as well as elements of prestige. These perils are as real as ignomy, exile or prison, even death, the frequent destinies of traditional intellectuals in Europe. And yet, the intellectual has usually enjoyed a veneration in Europe which scarcely has a parallel in the common American attitude toward those who take on the valiant role of questioner, critic, or intellectual trailblazer.''

What a problem it would be for the church, Wright added, if ''any who might be taken as her representatives in any sense of the world of the campus, the press, or the forum reveal contempt for that 'wild living intellect of man' of which Cardinal Newman spoke.''

So radically has the church changed with Vatican Council II (1962-1965) that it is impossible to imagine that 1950s debate occurring today. The Catholic intellect is free, and concern about orthodoxy is about the last thing worrying thinking Catholics nowadays. Still, what was the condition that gave rise to the anti-intellectualism that Cavanaugh and Ellis so accurately espied?

Perhaps the best analysis was provided by Professor Thomas F. O'Dea in his book *American Catholic Dilemma* (1961). O'Dea saw American Catholic intellectual life being hampered by five factors, as follows:

John Deedy

Formalism, or the strong attachment to the external forms and observances of religion, as distinct from a strong intellectual appreciation of faith itself;

Authoritarianism, or a readiness to accept positions and statements less on their intrinsic merits than on the authority of those enunciating them, from pope, to priest, to nun (this, in contradistinction to Thomas Aquinas, who regarded arguments from authority as the least persuasive of all);

Clericalism, or what now might be called ''creeping infallibalism''; i.e., the tendency of the clergy to assimilate errorlessness to their own person and to statements of their own, and a concomitant inclination on the part of the laity to accept this situation, so that clerical word became dogma, whatever the context;

Moralism, or the impulse to focus on the morality, or the rightness or wrongness of a particular reality, rather than on fact or truthfulness;

Defensiveness, the ''my church right or wrong'' syndrome, one which shut ears to legitimate criticism, that retreated from threatening controversy, and that indulged in protectiveness, even if it meant rewriting the record.

As said, we are talking here of history. So dramatically different is today's church that the conditions pinpointed by O'Dea are virtual artifacts of the American Catholic experience.

Facts, Myths and Maybes

Does this new condition make the American church a more intellectual place? Probably not, but it does make it far less a repressive or intellectually inhibiting a place—which is really all that the thinking Catholic asks. Will this benign condition endure? One would be tempted to say yes, if only because history is never reversed, at least not completely. But then new papacies come with new ideas, and that of John Paul II is not nearly so progressive as many expected a papacy would be almost of necessity in the aftermath of Vatican II. Is this reality a threat then to the church's intellectual standing? Perhaps yes, perhaps no. History has the definitive answer.

* * *

The church once held that the earth was flat.

MYTH . . . The church once held that the earth was the center of the universe, and that the sun and the rest of the solar system revolved around it rather than the sun. The concept was wrong-headed, and Galileo, if no other scientist, suffered from that wrong-headedness. But a motionless earth is a concept quite different from a flat earth.

Actually, as far back as the ancient Greeks, scholars believed the earth to be spherical. They didn't know how perfectly spherical, any more than they knew what exactly lay any great distance beyond the ocean horizons that the flimsy ships of the time were able to navigate. But they did believe the earth to be round.

Accept Jeffrey Burton Russell's proposition in his book, *Inventing the Flat Earth* (Praeger, 1991), and the flat-earth theory belongs to nineteenth-century invention, being fostered on this side of the Atlantic by Washington Irving's voluminous *Life and Voyages of Christopher Columbus* (1828), a quixotic skate between history and romance, and in Europe by the quirky French historian, Antoine-Jean Letronne, and his 1834 disquisition, ''On the Cosmographical Opinions of the Church Fathers.''

Leading Catholic thinkers, such as Augustine, the Venerable Bede and Thomas Aquinas, had all believed the world spherical, and theirs was representative church thought over the centuries. Isidore of Seville was an exception; he was ambiguous about the shape of the earth.

Actually, one has to go back to very early Christian centuries to find serious proponents of the flat-earth theory, and their work was so eccentric that it was shunted aside and forgotten until centuries later. Two of them—Lactantius, a third-century convert, and Cosmas Indicopleustes, a sixth-century Greek—were exalted as part of the nineteenth-century fixation, and became centerpieces in the flat-earth mythology laid against the church. Ironically, Lactantius had been posthumously condemned as a heretic, and Cosmas Indicopleustes' writings had been dismissed in his lifetime as unworthy, and were not even translated from Greek into Latin until 1706.

The nineteenth-century preoccupation with what the church thought on the subject was an appendage to the larger issue of evolution. The flat-earth theory was used by evolutionists to disqualify the church by pointing up the conflict, alleged or real, that existed between religion and science. According to Russell, "a body of false knowledge" was created by so-called experts who consulted "one another instead of the evidence."

* * *

The church is four-square opposed to evolution.

MYTH . . . From the beginning, evolution has been a Protestant preoccupation, not a Catholic one, as the famous Huxley-Wilberforce debate of 1860 at Oxford and the 1925 Scopes trial in Dayton, Tennessee, help dramatize. From the vantage point of history, the Catholic church, in fact, comes through rather well on the evolution issue. By staying above the fray in those early contentious decades of debate, and by not hurling thunder bolts, the church spared itself and its people a considerable amount of latter-day embarrassment.

Not that Rome has ever lovingly embraced the idea of scientific evolution. To the contrary.

John Deedy

Historically, Rome tended to regard Darwinian theory on the origin of species with great suspicion, even as dangerous. But, as said, there were no ringing condemnations from Rome, nor was there a rush to place evolutionary tracts on an already crowded Index of Forbidden Books. A provincial council of Cologne in 1860 rejected as contrary to Scripture and to faith the theory of "transformism"—that is, that man spontaneously sprang from some lower life form—and Vatican Council I (1869-1870) echoed that conclusion, although in low key. Similarly, in 1909 the Vatican's Biblical Commission, though refusing to question the literal and historical meaning of Genesis, which of course evolution had brought into doubt, ruled that one was not bound in belief to the exact word of Genesis and the creation story therein. The commission confirmed this in a 1948 letter to Paris' Emmanuel Cardinal Suhard, stating that the 1909 document was to be regarded "in no way a hindrance to further truly scientific examination of the problems in accordance with the results acquired in these last forty years."

Pius XII ratified that view in the 1950 encyclical *Humani generis*. Pius' approach was characteristically cautious. Materialism and pantheism were condemned, and moderation was counseled in any reinterpretation of Scripture. But evolution was recognized as a distinct possibility. "The teaching authority of the church," Pius said, "does not forbid that, in conformity with the present state of human sciences and sacred theology, research and discussions on the part of men experienced in both fields take place with regard to the theory of evolution."

Be it said, the church never had much problem with evolution in plant or animal life, for the good reason that Genesis did not presume to detail how many and in what forms and varieties individual plant and animal species were created by God. Thus it could accept the propositions of botanists and zoologists that certain species, rather than being directly created, resulted from some process of modification, be it struggle, variation or selection.

It is rather when evolution comes to *homo sapiens*, man and woman, that cautions quicken. There the church does not concede scientists the same propositions it does on the animal and plant levels.

The complication involving *homo sapiens* is that Genesis is again vague about the manner in which man and woman were formed, except to say that the Lord God formed Adam of the dust of the ground (Genesis 2:7) and then made Eve from a rib of Adam (Genesis 2:22). But that's enough for the church to be hesitant about science's explanations. In considering the human species, the church insists on transcending evolutionary views that may apply to animals and plants—

John Deedy

obviously so, because "man," humankind, possesses a property not found in other life forms: it has an immortal soul.

This still does not mean that the church has a closed mind on the possibility of an "evolved" human species. The so-called "missing link" from lower life to human species does not exist, or has not yet been found. Nonetheless, the church is willing to allow that data exist connecting bodily organism with the anthropoid ape. Accordingly, it leaves open the question of the evolution of the human species—*provided* it is believed that the human body was derived from other living matter, as distinct, say, from some happenstance emergence from slimy, single-cell algae or bacteria; *provided*, too, it is believed that humankind derived from one pair (Adam and Eve, say), into whom souls were individually breathed by God; *provided*, finally, it is allowed that evolution, whatever its historical frame work, took place under the dispensation of Divine Providence.

There likewise is insistence that every individual human soul, from the beginning of earthly history to the present and into the future, requires a special gift of existence from God.

With all these provisos, it is obvious that evolution is far from being canonically blessed. On the other hand, it is not excoriated. Evolution, in fact, is held to be consistent with Catholic Christian possibilities.

Facts, Myths and Maybes

The letter of the Bible puts the church in an ambivalent position on ecological issues.

OBVIOUSLY . . . Certainly the admonition to Adam and Eve to "increase and multiply; fill the earth and subdue it" (Genesis 1:27-28) makes it difficult for the church to address certain environmental questions. Take population. Factor into the biblical admonition church teaching on artificial birth control, and Catholics of given regions—the Far East, for example—are virtually neutralized in trying to cope with their area's most urgent problem, overpopulation. They can only repeat the church's position on population control: responsible parenthood, rhythm system, sexual abstinence. Beyond population numbers, there's the ambiguity of Genesis' instruction to "subdue" the earth. Is that the kiss of extinction to wetlands, mountain slopes, tropical rain forests, rolling plains? Is everything to be "subdued" or are some facets of nature to be preserved and protected? If so, what and how much?

On the positive side, however, there's the biblical paean that "The earth is the Lord's and the fullness thereof" (Psalms 24:1), and there's the New Testament emphasis on stewardship (Luke 16:1-8; 1 John 3:17-18), expressing a responsibility in a less literal age of biblical interpretation that extends not only to being thy brother's keeper, but the earth's as well. The logic is simple: if one wastes or otherwise abuses God's natural

resources, one is violating a trust, an implicit covenant
with God to be respectful of and responsible for his
(her?) creation.

The dilemma for Catholics is that it is virtually impossible to talk about living space and preservation of
the environment without being cast back to the subject of population control, and there the church is
almost automatically disadvantaged. When Pope Paul
VI in 1965 appealed before the United Nations "to
multiply bread so that it suffices the tables of mankind,
and not, rather, favor an artificial control of birth . . .
in order to diminish the number of guests at the banquet of life," ecologist Dr. Paul Ehrlich mockingly
countered: "We have already seen that the 'banquet
of life' is, for at least half of humanity, a breadline or
worse." Paul was an easy target, as any pope would
have been.

In *Nature Is a Heraclitean Fire,* a 1991 monograph on
the ecology in the series "Studies in the Spirituality
of Jesuits," Father David S. Toolan, S.J., speaks of concern for soil, water and air as the "ultimate pro-life
issue." It is, of course, and it just may be that the
church is beginning to accept that fact. In his 1989 visit
to Madagascar John Paul II added environmental and
wildlife preservation to his list of concerns, the first
real expression of ecological kind on record from a
pope, and in his lengthy World Peace Day message
of 1990 he described the ecological crisis as a moral

issue that "lays bare the depth of man's moral crisis." There have been returns to the topic since, but no encyclical, as some have urged; at least none yet.

Until there is an encyclical or other major pronouncement at highest levels, the church remains open to the charge of indifference—or worse, of being a body of cold, insensitive dogmatists in a world that too quickly could devolve into cesspool. The world is headed that way.

Consumer advocate Ralph Nader said not long ago: "The planet earth is a seamless structure with a thin slice of sustaining air, water, and soil that supports [some five] billion people. This thin slice belongs to us all, and we use it and hold it in trust for future earthlings. Here we must take our stand." Popes should be saying things like that, and if they did maybe peoples of the world would wake up to what is happening to planet earth.

* * *

The church has reimposed its ban against Catholics belonging to the Masons.

FACT . . . Freemasonry came under church ban in 1738, when Pope Clement XII (1730-1740) condemned the organization founded in 1717 as anticlerical and for alleged secret plotting against both church and state. The condemnation was reiterated by eight popes in seventeen separate pronouncements. However in 1974, while Paul VI (1963-1978) was pope, the Congregation for the Doctrine of the Faith under Franjo Cardinal Seper issued a letter interpreted to mean that Catholics might join Masonic lodges which were not anti-Catholic. In the U.S., if nowhere else, this appeared to open membership to Catholics, since American Freemasonry here was essentially a fraternal and humanitarian body. That opening was closed after John Paul II became pope. On February 17, 1981, the congregation termed the earlier interpretation erroneous. Two years later—November 26, 1983—the congregation reinstated the ban on Catholic membership with the approval of John Paul II. Its ruling:

"The church's negative position on Masonic associations . . . remains unaltered, since their principles have always been regarded as irreconcilable with the church's doctrine. Hence, joining them remains prohibited by the church. Catholics enrolled in Masonic associations are involved in serious sin and may not approach Holy Communion. Local ecclesiastical authorities do not have the faculty to pronounce a judgment on the nature of Masonic associations which might include a diminution of the above-mentioned judgment."

The one mitigation: unlike earlier condemnations, the ruling does not invoke or impose the penalty of excommunication. Neither does the new Code of Canon Law.

* * *

The church has made its peace with Rotary International.

FACT . . . although, as implicit in the statement, for years theirs was a negative relationship.

Rotary International was founded in 1905 as a world-wide fellowship of business and professional men (it now admits women) concerned about peace, social justice and community relations. Noble stuff.

For the bishops of Spain, however, Rotary was suspect, and in the 1920s they hung on it the tags of secularism and religious indifference. The allegations were echoed by bishops in Mexico, The Netherlands and several South American countries. Inevitably the word reached Rome, and Rotary found itself in disfavor there. In 1951 the Congregation of the Holy Office acted with the approval of Pope Pius XII (1939-1958). In January of that year it issued a decree banning all priests from membership in Rotary, adding that they weren't even to attend club meetings, a detail which effectively foreclosed acceptance of speaking invitations before the group. At the same time, Catholic laymen, though not warned away completely, were cautioned to observe the church's canonical provisions concern-

John Deedy

ing "secret, condemned, seditious and suspect" societies.

At the time *Osservatore Romano,* the Vatican daily, justified the move against Rotary in terms of its non-religious character and lay attitudes on matters of moral and social justice. The paper also professed to see Masonic (and presumably, therefore, anti-Catholic) influences in Rotary activities in certain countries. Rotary defended itself by saying it followed a policy of strict neutrality with regard to religion and in adhering to its motto, "Service, Not Self." Rome was not impressed.

That ban against Rotary was in effect for fourteen years. During that time, no U.S. bishop was reported as taking any action barring laymen from joining Rotary, but membership from the ranks of the American Catholic clergy was unheard of—unlike now, of course, when priest-membership is common.

The ban against Rotary ended with Pope Paul VI (1963-1978). He gave his implicit blessing to the group at a special audience of 1,500 Italian Rotarians at the Vatican on March 20, 1965. Paul confessed that reservations about Rotary had existed at the Vatican, but indicated they now belonged to the past. He said he was extremely interested in the aims and activities of Rotary, noting that these tend "to group together men of different confessions and ideas for the common good." Further, he declared it "gratifying" to see in

Facts, Myths and Maybes

Rotary members who were "ready to bring accents of the Christian message into its activity," so that "the Master of Humanity, Jesus Christ our Lord, is by no means an outsider among its ranks."

Embarrassing chapter closed.

* * *

The Knights of Columbus is a "secret" organization, but the church has never cautioned against it.

TRUE . . . But then the church is in on the secret.

* * *

Adam and Eve had no navels, bellybuttons, or did they?

NO SNICKERING . . . this is no riddle; whether Adam and Eve had navels was as serious a question for early theologians, as how many angels could occupy a single unit of space was for Thomas Aquinas.

Presumably neither Adam nor Eve would have an umbilicus or navel, as having been created by God (Adam from dust; Eve from a rib of Adam) rather than being born of woman, an umbilical cord would not have been involved in either event. The theologians decided, however, that Adam and Eve arrived as "finished" creations, and therefore since they came complete with heads of hair and fingernails, they also possessed navels.

311

John Deedy

The matter seems to have been settled well before the Renaissance, for Italian artists like Michelangelo and Masoccio, and, to the north, Lucas Cranach the Elder, were all depicting Adam and Eve with navels. No more fudging around with leafed branches, crossed arms and angled elbows. Reflect on Michelangelo's "The Creation of Adam" on the ceiling of the Sistine Chapel. The first point of reference is the forefinger of God and Adam touching one another; the second, Adam's masculinity; the third, Adam's navel.

Of course it could be argued that artists use models for their work, models come with navels, and therefore navels would then appear on the image of any naked person. Except navels could be brushed out, couldn't they, or overlooked, like some unpleasant skin blemish? No, the theologians had set the rule for the artist in the atelier.

But not forever. Darwinian discoveries quickened the issue of biblical literalism, and once again artists were running for cover on questions like navels on the first man and woman. If humankind evolved from the ape, the first pair would have had navels, to be sure. On the other hand, if the first pair was created . . . Back to fudging. Nineteenth-century illustrator John Tenniel thus put his Adam and Eve in high-slung boxer-type shorts. Others put Tarzan robes on Adam and full-bodied Dorothy Lamour type sarongs on Eve. Art had

Facts, Myths and Maybes

come full circle, if not theology—which by now wisely didn't seem to care, one way or the other.

* * *

Black patent leather shoes reflect upwards (old parochial-school saw).

TRUE . . . but only if they're shined.

INDEX

314

Index

Canon Law, code of, 61-2, 80, 145, 168, 169, 206, 223, 242-3, 271-2, 308
Canonization, 154-8, 244
Cantanei, Vannozza, 252
Canute, 152
Capitularies, 292
Cardinal, The, 198
Cardijn, Joseph, abbe, 186
Carroll, John, bishop, 131
Carthage, council of, 62
Casaldaliga, Petro, bishop, 247
Cassiodorus, 259
Carthage, council of, 12, 122
Catherine of Genoa, saint, 64
Catherine of Siena, saint, 256
Catholic Church, *ubique*
  as institution 114-6
  rites of, 117
Catholic Encyclopedia (1913), 58, 149, 178, 232, 248-9, 269, 292
Cavanaugh, John J., C.S.C., 295
Celibacy (clerical), 122-7
Celularius, Michael, patriarch, 27
Centesimus annus, 189
Chacon (Chaconius), 286
Chalcedon, council of, 104
"Challenge of Peace, The: God's Promise and Our Response," 190
Chang, Dr. M.C., 200
Charlemagne, 292
Christ, Jesus, *ubique*
Christus dominus, 230
Chordegang of Metz, 259
Christmas, 146, 275, 276-9, 280
Christopher, 152
Cicero, 260
Circumcision, feast of, 147-8, 280
Clavius, 286
Clement VII, pope, 274
Clement VIII, pope, 138
Clement XI, pope, 153
Clement XII, pope, 170, 270, 307
Clement of Ireland, 259
Clermont, synod of, 123
Cologne, council of, 302
Colors (liturgical), 173-5
Commandments (Decalogue), 18-20, 32, 34
Communion of the Saints, 106-8
Confirmation, 66, 67, 71-4
Conrad, emperor, 55
Congregation for the Causes of Saints, 157
Congregation for the Clergy, 79

Congregation for the Doctrine of the Faith, 203, 240, 263
Congregation for the Discipline of the Sacraments, 79
Congregation for Divine Worship, 76
Congregation for the Doctrine of the Faith (Holy Office), 210, 226-7, 308, 309
Congregation of Rites, 151
Congregation for the Sacraments and Divine Liturgy, 233
Conscience, freedom of, 12-3, 178-80, 182-5
  Guiding principle, 28-31, 205
Constance, council of, 141
Constantine I, emperor, 54, 196
Constantine V, emperor, 162
Constantine VI, emperor, 55
Constantinople, synod of (867), 26-7
Constantinople I, council of, 54
Constantinople IV, council of, 55
Constantinople, patriarch of, 26, 50
Constans ac sedula, 270-1
Corot, 90-1
Correns, Carl, 213
Councils, ecumenical, 54-7
Cosmas Indicopleustes, 300-1
Cranach, Lucas, the Elder, 312
Cremation, 223-7
Crisan, Traian, archbishop, 157
Crusades, 13, 27, 264-7
  Children's Crusade, 266-7
Cum sicut, 270
Cushing, Richard J., cardinal, 251
Cyprian, saint, 11

Damasus I, pope, 54
Dark Ages, 258-61
Dawson, William, 273
Deacons
  Permanent, 131-4
  Women, 134-7
Death, 86, 87-8
Descartes, René, 241
de Charny, Geoffrey, 273-4
De controversis, 241
"Declaration on Euthanasia," 220-1
"Declaration on Sexual Ethics," 203
Deicide, 180-2
Dei verbum (Dogmatic Constitution of Revelation), 42
de Paradis, Domenica, 256
de Mailly, Jean, monk, 140
Devil, 165-7

315

Index

Index

Index

318

Index

Index